GLOCK'S HANDGUNS

BY
DUNCAN LONG

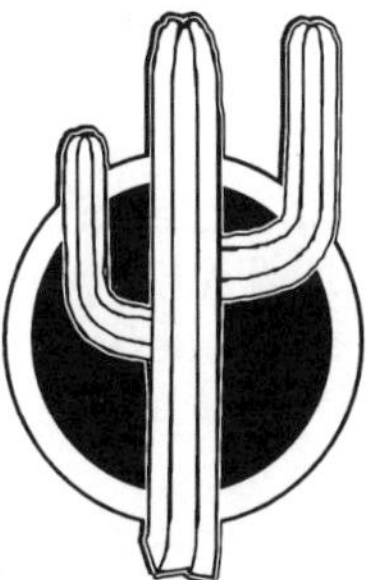

Desert Publications
El Dorado, AR 71731-1751 U. S. A.

Glock's Handguns

by

Duncan Long

Published by Desert Publications
215 S. Washington
El Dorado, AR 71730
info@deltapress.com
870-862-2077

ISBN 0-87947-152-2
10 9 8 7 6 5 4 3 2
Printed in U. S. A.

Desert Publication is a division of
The DELTA GROUP, Ltd.
Direct all inquiries & orders to the above address.

ACKNOWLEDGMENTS

Thanks must go to the many fine people at Glock, Inc., including former employees Al Bell and Robert W. Gates, II, along with Dave Shroka of Indelible, Inc.,as well as current employees including Wayne Holt, all of whom supplied manuals, photos, and catalogs over the last few years that it's taken to get this book up and running. Also very helpful was Glock fan George Guillory. And a thank you must also be given to the other companies listed in this book who supplied me with a wealth of photos, information, and sample products for the researching and writing of this book.

I must also express my gratitude to Larry Combs for railroading another book through and again working his magic on my manuscript (as well as the generous advance he arranged that helped keep bread on the household table during the writing of the book).

WARNING

Technical data presented here, particularly technical data on ammunition and the use, adjustment, and alteration of firearms, inevitably reflects the author's individual beliefs and experience with particular firearms, equipment, and components under specific circumstances which the reader can not duplicate exactly. The information in this book should therefore be used for guidance only and approached with great caution. Neither the author nor the publisher assumes any responsibility for the use or misuse of information contained in this book.

CONTENTS

Chapter 1

The Late Bloomer

Most firearms being manufactured worldwide are produced by old establishments which trace their lineage back to at least the 1800s; some European companies go back even further. Even the "new kids on the block", like the IMI (Israeli Manufacturing Industry) and Sturm, Ruger & Company can track their ancestry back nearly half a century. The few newer companies that exist often make only limited numbers of guns for the U. S. sporting market; and these enterprises usually bloom and wither like beautiful but short-lived summer flowers.

Glock Gesellschaft GmbH of Deutsch-Wagram, Austria, is an exception to this rule. The brain behind the company is Gaston Glock, an Austrian engineer who decided to put his designing skills toward the creation of a new firearm that would make use of modern industrial materials for easy manufacture and durability of the final product. But Glock didn't set out to make guns. He created his company in 1963 to produce office furniture and hardware. Eventually it strayed into producing police and military related products including military knives, hand grenades, machine gun belts, and entrenching tools.

Suddenly foreign businessmen were appearing on the front stoop of his 15-man factory, asking if the Glock Gesellschaft

Among Glock's products are excellent bayonets and fighting knives as well as a folding shovel that can also be employed as an ax or saw. (Photo courtesy of Glock, Inc.)

GmbH would take on the manufacture of their pistols. When Gaston Glock made some inquiries as to why everyone was suddenly interested in the fabricating pistols in Austria, he discovered that the Austrian military was searching for a new pistol to replace its aging P-38s (whose design was developed in the late 1930s). The catch to the specifications for the proposed military pistol was that manufacturer had to be Austrian in order to win the contract.

Seeing a potentially huge market, the inventor turned his skills toward creating a new pistol.

Now to say that Gaston Glock approached the creation of a new pistol without any preconceived notions would be an understatement. He would later tell reporters that he started his project in almost total ignorance about the operation of firearms. "In 1980, I didn't know the difference between a pistol and a revolver," he would later say. You can't start at a much lower level of knowledge.

But Glock was a quick learner. He also wasn't limited in the materials he could use in fabricating his new pistol. Because not only did he have experience in designing for tools made from everything from stainless steels to tough space-age plastics, the Austrian military had demonstrated its willingness to accept a radically new design. The rifle chosen in 1977 as the standard issue weapon for Austrian soldiers was none other than the "spacey" Steyr AUG ("Armee Universal Gewehr" or Army Universal Rifle).

The AUG was unorthodox from start to finish with a plastic receiver as well as a plastic trigger group and plastic magazines, all united in a bullpup stock with an integral telescopic sight and quick-change barrel. Any one of the features would have been innovative on a combat rifle in 1977; to have them all on one gun was truly a first. So it was apparent that the Austrian military would be open to any pistol design, no matter how revolutionary, provided it operated reliably. Glock had free rein to exercise his creativity.

In the 1980s, it was a safe bet that the Austrian military was open to new firearms designs, as demonstrated years earlier by the selection of the Steyr AUG as the standard military rifle. (Photo courtesy of Gun South, Inc.)

Nearly as surprising as the end pistol layout Gaston Glock and his engineering team created was the time he took to design the new pistol. After he and two employees had dissected every pistol they could lay their hands on, they had a design ready to go into production in only six months, an astoundingly short period even in today's "hi-tech" marketplace with computer-assisted designing and the like.

However, Glock wasn't totally happy with the results. He went, as the saying goes, back to the drawing boards and reworked the design. Two months later the gun the world came to know as the "Glock 17" was in operational, prototype form.

The tried and proven basic layout of the Glock pistols follows that which was pioneered by John Browning and other inventors during the early 1900s. This positions the magazine release to the rear of the trigger guard, the slide stop lever above the left grip, and the trigger ahead of the magazine well. Internally, the recoil spring rides below the barrel and the barrel uses a short recoil, breech lockup. (Shown here is the short barrel/grip version, the Glock 19.)

Of course the firearm was not entirely new. As with even the most radical of today's firearms' designs, it borrowed from the past.

First of all, it follows the tried and proven layout of most modern pistols with a side stop lever, magazine catch, trigger, and so forth in their more or less standard positions. The gun also has a detachable magazine with a conventional spring, like that of earlier designs.

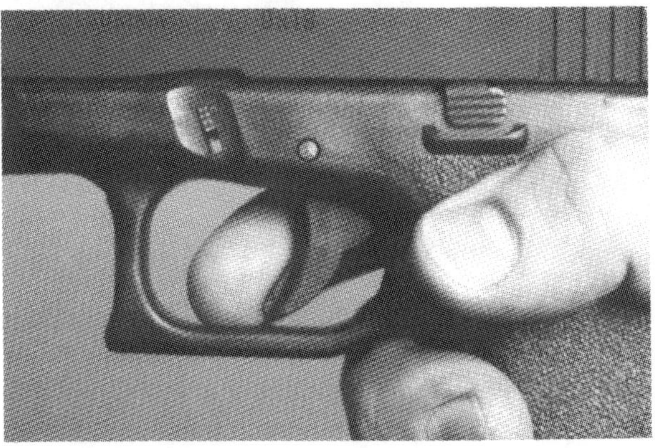

Most shooters find the "control" layout of the Glock very easy to use. And the trigger's manual safety can be "forgotten" without problem. (Photo courtesy of Glock, Inc.)

After searching through a variety of barrel lockup systems, Glock settled on the age-old High-Power design created by John Moses Browning during the 1930s and then used a slide locking system similar to that employed on the SIG Sauer P220. This short recoil, breech locked system has proven both safe and reliable over the years and is also tough enough to accommodate a variety of chamberings, something that's important to consider since shooters seem to be fickle when it comes to giving up one chambering for the "newest and most powerful" to come down the pike.

Gaston Glock borrowed the locking system for his pistol from the design pioneered by John Moses Browning in his High-Power pistol of 1935.

Top view of Glock 19 clearly shows the SIG Sauer-style lockup of the squared off breech-end of the barrel into a keyed slot in the slide.

The hammer/trigger mechanism exploited by most modern semiauto handguns presents a potential problem spot for modern pistols, especially military weapons that may be coated with mud or dropped in the sand in a variety of battlefield conditions. No doubt to avoid the likely ingress for dirt as well as to simplify his pistol design, Glock chose to do away with the hammer, instead adopting a striker that permitted both a simpler design as well as allowing the almost complete enclosure of the rear of the slide to prevent contaminants from entering the firearm from this point.

The idea of a striker-fired semiauto pistol was nothing new (although successfully marketing a gun with such a system was). One of the first viable systems was the Roth-Steyr Model 1908 which, though never a commercial success, was adopted by the Austro-Hungarian Army as a cavalry pistol.

Another striker-fired pistol that met with very limited success was the "Le Francaise" manufactured by Manufrance (Manufacture Francaise de Armes et Cycles de Saint Etienne, Sait Etienne, France). The company produced a whole family

One of the first viable striker-fired pistols was the Roth-Steyr Model 1908.

of striker-fired pistols starting with a diminutive 6.35mm model, the "Modele de Poche" that was marketed in 1914. Since these pistols all operated on the blow-back principle, none could accommodate the more powerful rounds like the 9mm Luger which were then becoming popular with military groups; the pistols fell to the wayside as other more robust designs replaced them.

Despite the fact that Glock recycled other older pistol designs, the end result wasn't anything like the previous features of the guns borrowed from. This was because Glock's specialty was working with new synthetic plastics which could be injection molded into a variety of shapes. Anything that could be formed of plastic was a candidate for that material rather than steel. And parts not suited for plastic were candidates for new rust-resistant alloys or the like with the Tenifer matte finish that appears on most models of the Glock pistols having greater corrosion resistance to salt water than does stainless steel.

The Tenifer finish is created through a carbo-nitrating hardening process, applied to the metal at 932 degrees Fahrenheit. This nitrate bath penetrates the metal surface of the slide and other parts for several thousandths of an inch, creating a "flake free" surface bonded into the metal. The hardness achieved with the Tenifer coat is truly amazing; it rates at 70C of the Rockwell Scale used with gem stones and metals. That means the only thing tougher than the Tenifer finish is a diamond. To add to the durability of the pistol, the Tenifer finish is next Parkerized, giving it even greater corrosion resistence.

A few metal parts on the pistol aren't Tenifer coated; these generally have a Parkerized finish and include the slide stop, extractor, extractor depressor plunger, trigger bar, ejector, and slide stop lever. The frame rails embedded in the frame are chrome steel. And all springs are unfinished steel for maximum strength.

Because of the heat necessary to apply the Tenifer finish, obviously it can't be reapplied to a pistol without damaging the hardness of the metal. But the Parkerized finish (which is what generally wears off) can be replaced by the manufacturer as well as many gunsmiths.

The barrel also shows some refinements which, though not unique to the Glock pistol, aren't seen in the majority of other firearms. The barrel is cold-hammer-forged with the rifling created through a hexagonal interior rather than through the traditional lands and grooves found in most bores.

This permits giving the bullet traveling down the barrel the proper spin for stabilization without creating excessive friction or permitting gas to leak past the bullet. This, in turn, translates into greater potential accuracy and a slightly increased muzzle velocity when compared to a barrel with lands and grooves. The design also improves barrel life and reduces fouling and overheating somewhat. While all of these improvements from the barrel design are minor and may not even be recognized by the majority of users, they still give another slight edge to the finished product. For added barrel life, the bore also gets a Tenifer finish during the manufacturing of the barrel.

The use of polygonal rifling and the Tenifer finish in the bore are reflected in the number of rounds some shooters have actually put through their Glocks. Gun writer Chuck Taylor recently fired 75,000 rounds though a Glock 17. This many rounds would wear away much of the rifling in the bore of most pistols and would be reflected by a widening of groups fired from the pistol. This wasn't the case during Taylor's test. He found his pistol still fired an average group of less than three inches from a Ransom Rest (target range: Thirty-five meters).

Glock pistols also have slightly greater muzzle velocity than pistols with grooves and lands having the same length of barrel. Because of this, the compact models of the Glock will actually have muzzle velocities equal to many pistols with barrels an inch longer than that on the smaller Glock.

When the prototype pistols started coming off the assembly line, it was obvious to even a casual inspection that the new Glock pistol was different from previous guns. The grip angle is racked back to that normally associated with target guns or "good pointers" like the Luger. And the trigger guard is large enough to accommodate a gloved finger--an important point for military and police buyers. The frame, grips, and trigger

Unlike most modern 9mm pistols, the Glock pistols have a steep grip angle similar to that of a target pistol. Shown here are the Glock 19 (bottom) and the Ruger Mark II target pistol (top).

guard are all one plastic molding, doing away with a variety of screws, plates, and other parts in the process--along with a lot of complicated machining. The magazine is also a plastic molding with a steel insert for added strength; inside the magazine there is a conventional steel spring to "power" it.

Glock also designed a variety of inexpensive but very tough injection molding holsters and magazine holders for the company's new pistol. These are molded to tightly hold the pistol or magazine. (More on these in subsequent chapters.)

To simplify manufacturing, some of the frame's metal parts are prepositioned in the mold before the plastic is injected around them. This makes fabrication easier and also does away with the need for pins or other systems normally needed to secure such parts to the frame. (With guns for the U. S. market, the serial number plate is also inserted into the mold ahead of the plastic; this assures that it is tightly bonded to the frame and nearly impossible to remove without damaging the frame itself, an important feature for governments wanting to keep strict control of firearms as well as to trace the source of those being employed by criminals.)

The frame has four steel inserts that the slide rails ride along; these inserts are hardened for maximum life. Employing four ultra-hard steel guides rather than long rails (as are used on many other semiauto pistols) adds to the dirt resistance of Glock's pistol. Dirt drops out of the pistol as the gun cycles. Had the gun had long rails, the dirt would be unable to escape easily and would bind the semiauto to the point that it could fail to function after being dropped in mud or sand.

Use of steel cross pins in the frame do away with any need for screws or similar fasteners; that said, only two pins are used with standard Glock pistols. One pin retains the trigger and slide latch and also helps anchor the barrel locking block; the

The use of four rail inserts in the frame (rather than the long rails found in most guns) makes Glock pistols very resistant to dirt--as demonstrated by military testing that included burying pistols in the sand and then firing them. Glock pistols normally do this without a hitch. (Photo courtesy of Glock, Inc.)

other pin at the upper rear of the grip holds the ejector and disconnector in place. (A third pin is found on large-caliber models of the Glock pistols. This pin transverses the frame just above the trigger pivot pin. This third cross pin secures the steel locking block to the frame during the heavier recoil of these guns).

The Heckler & Koch VP-70 with its polymer frame actually predated the use of a similar--but tougher plastic--on the Glock 17 frame.

Many people think the Glock was the first pistol to employ a polymer plastic for its frame. In fact the Heckler & Koch VP-70Z had utilized this system in 1970 along with a trigger system that was somewhat similar to the Glock's in operation. The VP-70Z was much bulkier than the Glock pistols however and also designed to be employed with a stock as a machine pistol as well as in its conventional pistol mode. Consequently the VP-70Z never saw any great acceptance except among a very limited number of police and civilian users where it was carried in its semi-auto form only, without the detachable stock and burst-fire mechanism.

The polymer chosen by Glock for his pistol frames was one he had invented. Dubbed "Polymer 2", it doesn't have the hard finish of a metal frame, but has other qualities that make it more ideal than metal for use as a gun frame.

First of all it is lightweight, weighing 14 percent less than steel--an important consideration with a gun that might be carried for 12 hours at a stretch by police or military personnel. At the same time the polymer has a tensile strength that is 17 percent stronger than steel, making the frame even more durable than what one might expect of an alloy or even steel frame. Additionally the plastic remains strong up to 392 degrees Fahrenheit or down to minus 75 degrees Fahrenheit.

In short, the polymer employed for the frame of the Glock pistol has a lot of important design pluses.

The slide assembly and barrel on the Glock pistols are little different from those of more conventional modern pistols. But there's one important difference: No manual safety is to be found on the frame or slide. Instead there's a small secondary lever that acts as a manual safety on the trigger itself, arguably making it a bit dubious as a "manual safety" in the ordinary sense of things. (This type of trigger safety is not entirely new; a similar design appeared on the Sauer "Behordenmodell" pistol.)

A passive firing pin block, which makes it impossible for the gun to fire without the trigger being pulled back into the fire position, augments the trigger safety. Glock pistols have a third safety in the form of a block that prevents discharge of the gun even when it's dropped from 6 feet onto a concrete surface or steel plate.

Take-down of the Glock is also extremely simple. The user just removes the magazine and checks the chamber to be sure the gun is empty, then pulls the trigger, and pulls back slightly on the slide. He then pulls down the slide locks located in depressions on either side of the frame. That done, the slide and barrel can be removed for cleaning. And for armorers, the only tool needed to take the entire mechanism apart is a small punch or even just an old nail.

Thanks to injection moldings and a simplified trigger/striker assembly, the entire gun is comprised of only 33 parts--including the magazine and sights; this is roughly half the number found in most other modern semiauto pistol designs. This reduction of parts along with the inexpensive injection molding of the frame, trigger, magazine catch, and magazine body promised a firearm that would be readily affordable as more and more of the pistols were produced on the company's automated machinery.

(It should be noted that the 33-part count has been "fudged" a little by the Glock publicity department. A careful

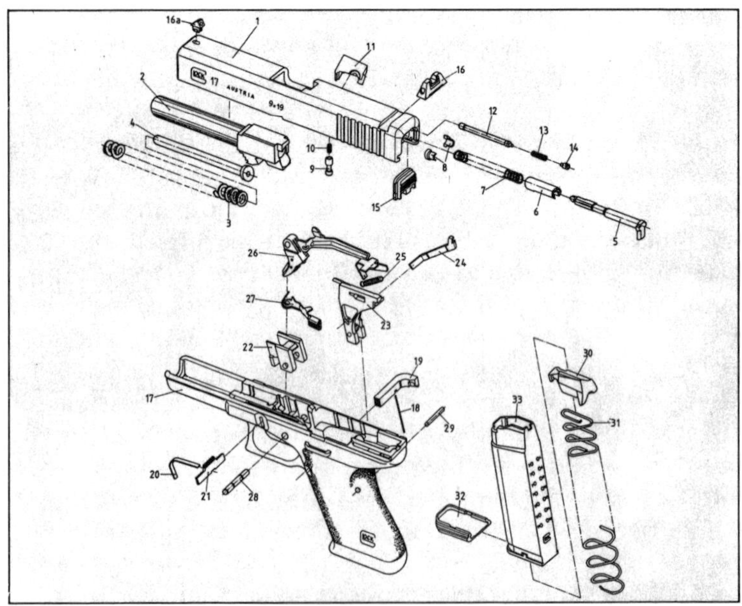

Exploded diagram of an early-model Glock 17 shows the simplicity of its design and a minimal number of parts when compared to other modern pistols. (Drawing courtesy of Glock, Inc.)

examination of the gun shows that some parts that are duplicated are counted only once--even though two are used with the gun--and some are also assemblies of several parts that can't be separated. When these are taken into consideration, the total parts count is closer to 35 or 36. But that's still a very low number for even the most modern of guns and smaller by about 20 or 30 parts when compared to most of its competitors.)

Gaston Glock's new pistol was awarded the inventor's seventeenth patent. The inventor's selection of a name was therefore simple: "Glock 17." This name has caused untold confusion as more models were fielded. Many shooters and even some firearms writers assumed that the pistol was named after the number of rounds its magazine held. This made sense when the gun was first fielded but became glaringly wrong as new guns were marketed with conflicting magazine sizes and model numbers.

Once Glock had pistols running in limited numbers of assembly lines, sample pistols were submitted for the Austrian military tests. While the specifications set down by the Austrian government required that the competition be limited to Austrian designs, the tests were far from easy. The grueling trials involved a total of five manufacturers' arms and consisted of firing 150,000 rounds through each pistol in a variety of conditions from extreme heat and cold to burying the guns in mud or sand and then retrieving and firing them.

Pistols were sprayed with water while being fired; they were frozen at minus 40 degrees Celsius for 12 hours and fired. They were subjected to high heat and then fired. Pistols were even supposed to be capable of being fired with a bullet already lodged in the bore without fragmenting the barrel (though not necessarily continuing to operate after such a disastrous occurrence). And the guns were required to work with any 9mm Luger cartridge, not just those designed for use by military pistols, an especially strenuous requirement since the nose and power configuration of ammunition seen in today's marketplace varies greatly.

Pistols in the Austrian military tests were subjected to grueling tests including wide temperature extremes and a variety of dirt and muck. (Photo courtesy of Glock, Inc.)

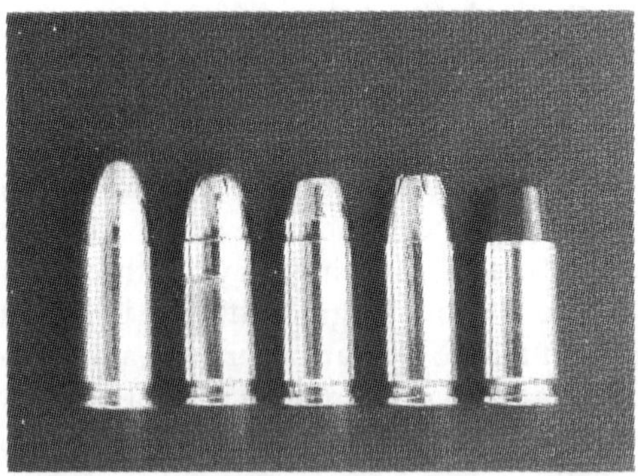

Pistols in the Austrian military tests also had to be able to function with any type of 9mm Luger ammunition currently being manufactured. (Photo courtesy of Glock, Inc.)

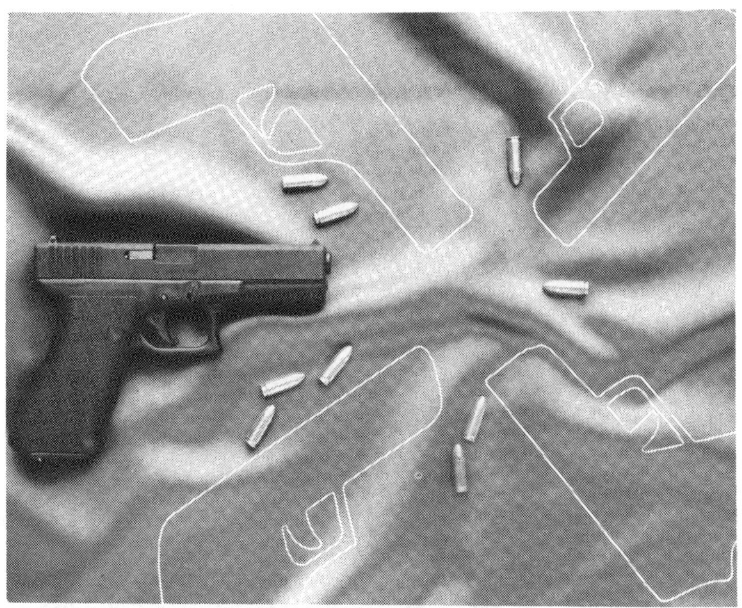

The Glock pistol eventually won out over its competition. Shown here are the four "police chalk outlines" of the Glock's competitors along with the winning pistol. (Photo courtesy of Glock, Inc.)

Though the Glock 17 was competing against eight firearms produced by five different seasoned companies with flocks of designers, the fledgling pistol proved the equal and more to any and all of its competitors. In fact, neither of the two Glock 17s submitted to the tests had any parts breakage or need for replacement parts and both stayed with the accuracy specifications of the test (ten shot groups within 2.75 inches at 25 meters). Each Glock pistol fired 150,000 rounds and continued to function properly.

By 1983 the Glock had won the competition and tests, besting its nearest competition, the Steyr GB. The Austrian government ordered 28,000 of the guns and Glock Gesellschaft GmbH was a viable gun manufacturer. After field trials the Austrian

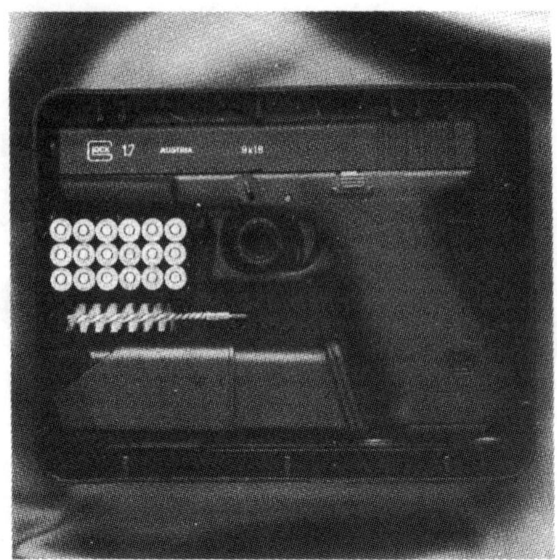

Glock 17 in its "issue" box containing everything a trooper needs: Cleaning kit, spare magazine, magazine loader, and even 18 rounds of ammunition. (Photo courtesy of Glock, Inc.)

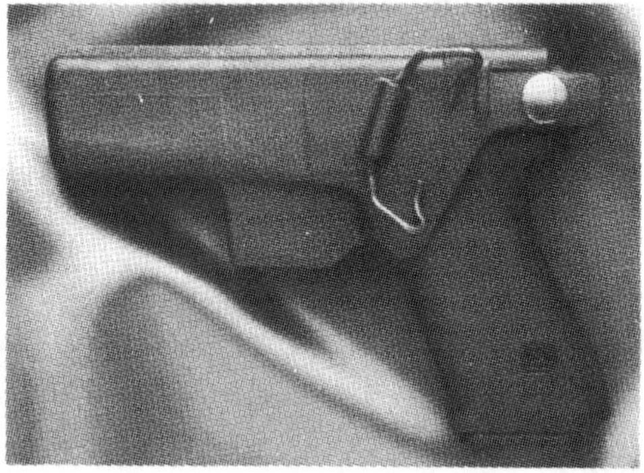

Glock 17 in its military holster. Like much of the pistol, the holster takes advantage of polymer for maximum toughness and low manufacturing costs. (Photo courtesy of Glock, Inc.)

government continued to be impressed and in 1985 made the Glock 17 its official firearm, designating it as the "P80" (reflecting the year in which the original government specifications for the pistol were laid down for military trials). Amazingly the guns that would be delivered to the Austrian military were virtually identical to the first prototypes Gaston Glock had created after only seven months of work, starting from scratch with almost no knowledge about firearms.

The Ministry of Defense (Bundesministerium fur Landesverteidgung) was soon disposing of its old Walther P38 pistols at the rate of 2,500 per year for the next three years, replacing them with the new Glock 17s. Later the Ministry of Defense would also replace its aging Colt 1911A1 .45 pistols with the Glocks as well.

In 1984 the new Glock 17 was introduced into the NATO tests of current production pistols. While no single pistol was

The Glock 17 in "rapid fire." Note ejected cartridge over pistol and the minimal muzzle rise due to design of the firearm which places the barrel axis low in the shooter's hand. (Photo courtesy of Glock, Inc.)

chosen as the gun for all NATO forces, the tests did prove to be eye openers to many smaller countries that had been buying guns from larger NATO members or who were shopping for replacements. Soon Norway and then Sweden had placed orders for the Glock 17 pistols and other countries were quickly following suit, especially those wanting a quality gun for special forces, palace guards, or the like. Soon Glock 17s were to be seen all around the world, from at the belts of the Canadian Royal Mounted Police, to the German anti-terrorist unit GSG 9, to the Presidential Guards in the Philippines.

Although Glock was invited to submit pistols to the U. S. XM9 tests being conducted by the U. S. Military in 1984 in order to select a new service arm, the Austrian manufacturer declined. The reason was quite simple. Gaston Glock had designed his pistol to comply with the Austrian requirements; meeting some of the U. S. specifications would require redesigning some features of the Glock pistol as well as retooling to produce it. The Glock 17 didn't enter the contest.

As Glock's company expanded, he resisted the temptation to use sub-suppliers, a practice many other companies employ when large government contracts are secured. Instead he hired more workers, expanding his staff from 15 to 40, while investing heavily in computer-controlled machinery to keep his parts precisely sized. And because everything on his pistols was being manufactured "in-house," Glock maintained a high level of uniformity and quality with the pistols his factory produced. Even today, only the springs and raw material are purchased from outside the factory; everything else is created inside.

Glock's design proved to be more flexible than other pistols when it came to meeting the specifications laid down in Government tests. The color of the pistol, for example, could be easily varied by changing the dye in the plastic frame and mating it to a similarly colored Tenifer coating on the slide and other metal parts.

The basic design also permits changes that are other than cosmetic. The trigger design, for example, can be easily modified to accommodate a wide range of pull weights that, unlike with many other pistols, are easily accomplished without dangerous modifications to the sear. By simply changing a part, an armorer can modify the weight of the pull needed to fire the gun from a few pounds to as much as 8 pounds or more, making the gun more suitable for policemen trained with double-action, heavy trigger-pull revolvers.

By modifying the injection molds, it would also be possible to modify the grip angle of the pistol since the rear of the frame behind the magazine well was simply plastic (unlike most other pistols which crammed this space with a heavy spring to power the hammer). This would make it possible to adjust the grip angle to the tester's needs, with angles anywhere from the standard "target pistol" style to the steeper angle used by traditional pistols like the High Power, Beretta 92, Colt 1911 and others. (It should be noted that most shooters prefer the original Glock 17 grip angle so no such modifications have been made to date by Glock.)

Because they lack a hammer and hammer spring, Glock pistols have an open, hollow area at the rear of the grip. This permitted the manufacture to create a grip angle suited to natural "pointing" to quickly bring a gun on target.

Most shooters find the Glock trigger pull easy to get used to, in part thanks to both its low weight of pull (with the exception of guns modified for government and police issue where there is concern with avoiding accidental shootings through inadequate training). Another important plus is that the Glock pistol's pull is consistent from one shot to the next, thanks to its striker design that avoids the use of a hammer.

While the Glock trigger pull has been called almost anything from a "two stage military pull" to a "double-action only" system by various gun writers (present author included); BATF and the Federal Law Enforcement Standards Testing Laboratory both also classify the Glock trigger as a "double-action" design. To keep things confusing, Glock advertising literature dubs the trigger a "Safe Action."

In fact most of these descriptions, with the exception of Glock's, don't really apply to the pistol since it lacks the traditional hammer assembly. With most semiauto pistols, only the first shot will be "double action" during which the hammer is both lifted and dropped to fire the gun as the trigger is pulled. After that first shot (or with all the shots in older semiauto designs), the hammer will remain back and all subsequent shots are fired from a shorter, lighter single-action pull that only drops the hammer.

Thus, with most semiauto pistols, there's a double-action pull (that brings the hammer through two positions) and a single-action pull (that only drops the hammer). And the difference in both the length of pull as well as the weight of pull needed to release the hammer between these two actions can be very unsettling to beginners who often accidentally squeeze off a shot when they think the weight of the first double-action pull will remain constant with subsequent shots--but it doesn't.

The Glocks did away with this change-of-pull problem. The weight of Glock's pull is consistent from the first to the last shot. And they also don't require that the shooter fuss with the hammer, being sure it is back when a shot is to be fired or forward and/or a safety engaged when the gun is going to be carried. When the shooter is finished with the Glock, simply removing the finger from the trigger guard puts the gun into its safe mode. There's no safety to fool with and no hammer to drop. This, too, reduces the likelihood of an accidental shooting and also prevents the specter of having an officer trying to fire his gun during a critical moment, only to discover the gun won't function because an awkward-to-operate safety has been left engaged.

The lack of a safety coupled with the consistent weight and length of pull became an important selling feature of the Glock pistols. Soon other manufacturers were striving to copy its features, even with guns designed around hammer operation. This has led to a variety of modifications of semiauto handguns including the removal of the manual safety on semiautos that originally had such a device, as well as models that fire only from the double-action position with a bobbed hammer dropping after each shot. By and large these guns have met with so-so acceptance, principally because the modifications are somewhat of stop-gap measures with trigger pulls remaining heavy and long because raising the hammer takes a lot of mechanical work. For this reason the Glock has remained in the lead with many such contests for buyer acceptance.

Glock's trigger design has also worked against the pistol. Obviously when military or police requirements spell out the need for a manual safety, the safety located on the Glock's trigger may, or may not, meet the requirements depending on how the specifications for the test are written.

When Glock's pistols were first introduced to the U. S. marketplace, some potential government buyers expressed the fear that the lack of any external manual safety other than the one on the trigger, coupled with the low pull weight required to fire the pistol, would result in a greater number of accidental discharges with police forces adopting the Austrian pistols. In fact, most departments (including both the Washington and New York City police departments) saw no increase in the rate of accidents when compared to what had occurred with the revolvers previously carried by officers. And some, like the Miami Police Department, actually saw a lower rate of accidental discharges with the Glock pistols.

In poorly trained police departments there have been claims that the trigger pull has caused accidental discharges. Such claims are hard to prove or disprove and, unfortunately, those investigating are often more inclined to blame the firearm rather than one of their fellow members. There are a couple of simple solutions that prevent such accidental discharges in the rare circumstances that they might occur.

The most effective is to simply instruct shooters to keep their trigger finger out of the trigger guard unless they need to fire the gun. Shooters never discover that they can't fire a pistol because they failed to get their finger to the trigger; in times of emergency, the subconscious makes sure that finger is on the trigger.

But the reverse isn't true.

When there's potential danger and the finger is on the trigger, it's possible for the gun to be accidentally fired. This situation can, of course, happen anytime that the user trips over or runs into an object (a common occurrence both on the battlefield as well as in the dark environments in which much police action takes place). It's doubly apt to happen when a soldier, policeman, or home owner has adrenaline racing through his veins at the prospect of facing an armed enemy. In such an instance, the muscles often jerk spasmodically and what seems like a small tightening of the trigger finger may actually be a pull strong enough to fire a weapon. For this reason, the expedient of keeping the finger out of the trigger guard is an essential habit that must be cultivated among anyone who carries a firearm.

The second solution, and one which unfortunately appeals to many bureaurocrats more than does spending money for the adequate training of recruits, is to increase the trigger pressure needed to fire a pistol. With Glock pistols, this is easily accomplished by substituting a stronger spring for the standard spring. And while this does reduce the chances of an accidental shooting somewhat, it unfortunately doesn't do away with the problem as well as does adequate training. In fact, many shooters will get into the habit of "taking up the slack" of the trigger to make it possible to get off a first shot more quickly if it's needed. And this, coupled with adrenaline that upsets the ability to "know one's own strength" creates an accidental shooting looking for a place to happen. Nevertheless, many "heavy trigger" kits are installed in Glock pistols worldwide, especially in areas that are more interested in turning out recruits in a hurry rather than adequately training them to do a proper job.

Currently there are five commonly seen trigger pulls with the Glocks. One is the standard 5-pound pull found on the majority of guns. The second is the 3.5 to 4.5-pound pull that's standard for the "L", long-slide target pistols (more on this variant of pistol in a bit). The third pull is a hefty 8-pounder; this is most commonly seen on smaller "hide out" versions of the Glock and is often selected by police departments concerned about accidental discharges of weapons. All three of these pulls are created by various configurations of the trigger connector.

The connector cams the trigger bar downward during the rearward pull of the trigger. When the rear edge of the trigger bar disengages the lug of the striker, the striker flies forward, hitting the primer and firing the cartridge. By changing the angle of the connector, the camming action changes, causing more or less pressure to be necessary to pull back the trigger. Thus the shape of the connector determines the weight of the trigger pull.

Two other trigger pulls are offered by Glock. These are both known as the "New York" pulls since they were created for police departments in that state. These are achieved by replacing the coiled spring normally seen in Glock pistols with a plastic spring that levers itself against the sear plate of the trigger. In theory, the New York spring feels more like a revolver trigger pull, the idea being that this similarity will aid in switching officers from revolvers to the new Glock pistols. This pull is seen in two weights: The standard 8-pound "New York Trigger" as well as the "New York +" which has a pull of 11 to 12 pounds.

Some writers and Glock users have mistakenly assumed that only the trigger spring determines the weight of pull; this simply is not true in all cases--though (just to keep things confusing) it is true with the "New York" and "New York Plus." The original 8-pound connector was created for the Metro Dade Police Department in Florida which wanted a less-easily fired pistol. And, obviously, the "New York" trigger pulls were created for police departments in that state.

It's possible to determine to some extent what the weight of a pull is by looking at the top portion of the connector that is exposed when the slide is removed from a Glock pistol. Connectors with no markings on the exposed tab are either the standard 5-pound pull or have a New York or New York Plus spring in place (if the pull seems heavy); these guns have a connector with the original 90-degree angle to them.

Connectors with a "-" are light "L" pulls in the three to four pound range with a sub-90-degree bend. Connectors with a "+" have the 8-pound pull achieved with a 105-degree angle to the connector.

Because the weight of pull can be modified by exchanging connectors, a Glock-certified armorer can quickly and inexpensively modify a Glock pistol with the cost of the replacement connector running only a few dollars. Any exchanges of the connector should only be done by a Glock-certified armorer. Putting the wrong parts together, as say, an 8-pound connector and a New York spring, can create a dangerous situation.

Regardless of the weight of pull, Glocks have a pull that "takes up the slack" for about 0.4 inch. This is followed by a heavier pull leading to discharge; this second portion of the pull generally covers about a half inch of travel. With the New York or New York Plus spring in place, the feel of the pull changes giving the illusion that the pull is similar to that of a revolver, rather then having the two stage feel of the original Glock pistols.

No matter which connector or trigger spring is being used, the striker itself is normally "semi-cocked" and in a rearward position before the trigger is pulled. Once the striker is released, it is brought back to its semi-cocked position by the cycling of the slide.

This system also permits very fast strings of shots for those familiar with the gun. Because the first half of the cocking of the striker is done by the action of the slide, it isn't necessary to return the trigger to its full-forward position before another shot can be squeezed off. The shooter only has to ease the trigger forward to where it would be after the first half of its return forward. From there pulling back on the trigger will fire another shot.

Generally the greatest accuracy will be realized on Glock pistols having lighter trigger pulls. As pull weight is increased, police and military users have seen shooters scores go down. Consequently those interested in maximum accuracy should consider having the lightest practical pull they feel comfortable with on their Glock pistol.

Most Glocks have a hole at the lower rear of the grip; some shooters have speculated that this is for use in mounting a stock to the gun, using the open space in the rear of the grip and the hole to somehow attach a military style stock to the firearm. In fact this is totally wrong, the hole was part of the original Austrian military requirements.

The hole is designed to be employed for fastening a lanyard to the pistol. Unlike most other lanyard arrangements on other firearms, this one didn't necessitate any extra parts or result in a nub that sticks down and gets in the way when loading magazines into the firearm. While a little care has to be exercised with lanyards (they can get a shooter tangled up or even stray into the action of the gun when it's cycling), the cord can be useful to those carrying a pistol near the water or in a situation where it might easily get lost or be "snatched" from the owner.

One thing has remained constant despite the many variations that have sprung up from the original Glock 17. The pistols have remained simple to manufacture and maintain as well as easy to operate, low-cost, and robust. This, coupled with the low initial cost of the pistols has made them first choice for a variety of buyers, from individuals to military and law enforcement agencies.

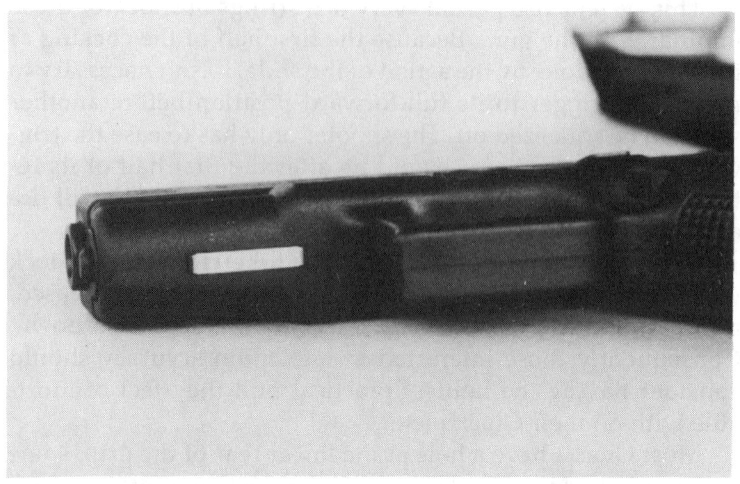

Glock pistols imported or assembled in the U. S. must have a metal serial number place in the lower, front of their frames.

All the pluses of Gaston Glock's pistol doesn't mean everything has been smooth for his marketing department, however. In 1985, Glock submitted a proposal to export his pistols to the U. S. Before it could get a permit, the guns had to meet with BATF (Bureau of Alcohol, Tobacco, and Firearms) approval. After inspecting the pistols, the agency made two requirements for pistols entering the U. S.: The guns would have to have a serial number plate embedded in the plastic of their frame and they would also have to have adjustable rear sights. (The latter requirement is an oddity that demonstrates the strange twists U. S. gun laws have taken. Although the U. S. Constitution provides that citizens have the right to own military weapons, BATF maintains that only sporting guns can be imported into the U. S. while military guns cannot be. In order to become a "sporting" arm, the Glock pistol has to have an adjustable sight.)

Gaston Glock made the needed changes with the design of a new sight being carried out in just a few days. Glock's factory quickly retooled to meet the BATF requirements and an American subsidiary, "Glock, Inc.", was set up in Smyrna,

Glock, Inc. plant, located in Smyrna, Georgia. (Photo courtesy of Glock, Inc.)

Current production Glock 17 showing adjustable rear sight required by U. S. BATF in order for the gun to be imported into America. (Photo courtesy of Glock, Inc.)

Georgia. This branch company would be in charge of marketing to the lucrative police and civilian markets in the U. S. Despite the securing of importation licenses and manufacturing okays by the company, the plans to produce guns in the plant in 1987 quickly came to a standstill.

The delay was caused by the anti-gun movement which was just getting into full swing. When they learned of the new gun's approval by BATF, liberal Congressmen and shady newsmen were "warning" the public about the new, "all plastic guns" that were being brought into the U. S. The public was told that the new pistols go through airport metal detectors. Worse yet, the story ran, Libya had purchased untold numbers of the new guns, no doubt to wreak havoc on the West with terrorist activity.

Soon the non-shooting public was totally confused and anti-gunners were testifying before the U. S. Congress that the Glock pistols had no legitimate purpose whatsoever; the guns were, according to these spokesmen, only useful to terrorists and would never be owned by anyone else. The evening TV news programs and more liberal publications beat the anti-Glock drum louder, sending the message that mankind must unite to ban these pistols if the free world was to remain safe.

Eventually saner individuals got their chance to rebut the hysterical calls for weapons bans. Officials from both the FAA and BATF testified that the pistols weren't a problem. Glock, Inc., produced X-ray photos of their pistols which, in the gun magazines that printed them (national media magazines never did), showed quite clearly that the Glock would be detected by airport security machines since the firearms, except for the polymer frame, were eighty percent steel. Likewise, airport metal detector manufacturers, angered by the misinformation the anti-gun lobby had propagated, demonstrated that their equipment had no trouble discovering a concealed Glock pistol, whether on a traveler's person or in his luggage, assembled or disassembled.

Gaston Glock himself, accompanied with Wolfgang Riedl, his marketing manager, and Karl Walter (the head of "Glock, Inc."), traveled to Washington and talked to anyone who would listen, showing the pistol, dismantling it, and explaining that Libyan purchases of the gun had never occurred.

To save face, the liberal media ignored Glock's demonstrations and moved on to another story; Congress passed a law outlawing plastic guns--should anyone ever figure out how to make such a thing (arguably impossible with today's technology). Soon the anti-gun groups, newscasters, and rabid politicians turned to assault rifles as the new "terrorist weapons" (even less likely to be used in the commission of a crime than handguns) to ban. And most ironically, some of the law enforcement personnel, conned into testifying for a ban of the Glock pistols as "guns only terrorists would have any use for," were soon wearing the pistols on a daily basis because their departments soon adopted the firearms.

Perhaps the most embarrassing event occurred in New York City where, at the height of the hysteria, city officials had

X-ray photo clearly shows the metal parts in a Glock. Obviously this firearm isn't the "plastic gun" hysterical gun-control opponents in the U. S. claimed it to be. (Photo courtesy of Glock, Inc.)

banned the Glock, declaring it so dangerous that it was a "prohibited weapon" alongside mortars and machine guns. No one, not even the fortunate few with pistol permits, could carry a Glock pistol in the Big Apple, according to the law of the city.

Then, in October, 1988, New York Police Commissioner Benjamin Ward was seen in public with a Glock pistol holstered on his belt. The Associated Press broke the story and the New York Post and New York Times quickly put it in their publications. Rather than jail the police chief, city fathers hastily called a commission meeting and decided to remove the Glock pistol from the "forbidden" list. A short time later, New York's finest were being issued Glock pistols to wear openly.

While in the U. S. to head off the "anti-plastic-terrorist-gun mania", Gaston Glock impressed many gun writers with his ability to dismantle and reassemble his firearms using only a small punch, nail, or whatever tool happened to be available. The inventor could rapidly take his pistol apart and reassemble it without any special tools or vises, something impossible with most firearms.

Since the pistol's survival of the anti-gun crowd, it has achieved a reputation that borders on the legendary. The Miami Police Department, for example, decided to test two Glock 17s for possible selection as a duty gun. The two guns were loaded and buried in sand; after being dug up, both fired flawlessly. They were reloaded and placed in buckets of sea water, left for 50 hours, removed, shaken free of water, and fired. No malfunctions. After Miami ordered Glock 17s for its officers, the two test guns were given to police instructors who still carry them and claimed to have put 50,000 rounds through each--without any parts breakage.

The Glock pistols have proven to be popular both with military as well as police and civilian shooters. In North America, for example, over half of the police departments switching from revolvers to semiauto pistols have chosen the Glock as their sidearm. By 1992, over 4,000 federal, state, or local law enforcement agencies were issuing Glock pistols to duty officers.

Many police officers, familiar only with revolvers, have little relish for switching to what they see as a "complicated semiauto pistol." And in the past such feelings have been justified when officers were suddenly presented with a weapon that switched from double- to single-action pull after the first shot, had a manual and/or hammer drop lever that had to be operated with the thumb, and seemed overly complicated.

This hasn't been true with the Glocks.

Officers only needed to learn how to load the magazine and cycle the slide. From there on all they had to know was how to pull the trigger. Range scores in most police departments went up by 50 percent when switching from revolvers to the Glock and many officers expressed a feeling of greater confidence on the job since they had a pistol with 15 to 19 rounds in it (depending on the chambering and magazine configuration) instead of only six cartridges, as with their old revolvers.

Obviously much of the acceptance of the Glock pistol has to do with the low price tag and high durability of the guns. However some of it has to do with pure showmanship as well.

For example, on Saturday, May 19, 1990, Glock, Inc., conducted a military-style torture test that demonstrated the durability of its pistols. The test began with the complete disassembly of twenty Glock 17 pistols. The parts were shuffled around and a pistol assembled of parts collected from the table without any regard to which gun they had originally belonged to. The pistol was then fired.

And fired.

And fired.

Not only did this randomly assembled gun continue to function flawlessly, it fired 4,500 rounds before there was any part failure: The breakage of the trigger spring. This part was replaced and more ammunition put through the gun, with only a pause to move targets up and down the range and a perfunctory cleaning of the gun every 2,500 rounds. After four hours of shooting, 10,140 rounds were put through the gun with the trigger spring being the only part to break.

While arguably a lot of other manufacturers might conduct such a demonstration with similar results, many probably wouldn't dare to do so publicly. Their firearms aren't that consistently durable. And even those who have trustworthy

Disassembled Glock 17s before Glock, Inc.'s "torture test" of May 19, 1990. One gun was assembled from randomly chosen parts and fired for over 10,000 rounds with only the failure of the trigger spring. (Photo courtesy of Glock, Inc.)

products still don't do such publicity stunts for fear something might go awry. But Glock, Inc., does conduct such demonstrations from time to time and the publicity pays off with shooters remembering the coverage and the demonstration of durability and reliability.

As sales of Glock pistols continue to climb worldwide, Glock Ges.m.b.H. has expanded its Ferlach facility where the guns are actually made. By mid-1993 the original factory had doubled in size and it appears that it will expand even more in the near future. And things also continued to expand in the U. S. as well.

The first guns brought into the U. S. by Glock, Inc., were manufactured and assembled in Austria. But by mid-1990, Glock, Inc. had a 43,000 square foot production facility created to assemble and test fire pistols from parts made in Austria.

This greatly speeded up the process of putting guns into the marketplace and also reduced the cost of the guns since American labor was somewhat less expensive than Austrian. The new plant helps avoid delays in delivery of guns when the Austrian plant received large government orders and also could get around possible future import restrictions the U. S. government might set up on importing foreign-made firearms.

Worldwide, new sales offices have opened in most large countries including France and Great Britain. And in the U. S., Glock, Inc., has even promoted its GSSF (Glock Sport Shooting Foundation) which organizes contests for owners of Glock pistols.

Glock, Inc., also created an armorer school which teaches police and military armories, free of charge, how to maintain Glock pistols as well as adjust and replace parts in them. (While the reliability of Glock pistols might seemingly make the job of an armorer much like that of a Maytag repairman, the fact that police and other institutional users aren't always too careful with their firearms undoubtedly makes up for the basic toughness of the firearm in terms of abuse and parts loss.)

Some gun manufacturers give certification to anyone who simply attends their classes; if the would-be armorer is still breathing when he leaves, he becomes certified. Perhaps in keeping with its Teutonic background, Glock, Inc., doesn't hand out certificates so freely. Those attending classes have to take a final exam to be sure they really learned what they need to know to work on the company's guns in the field. And certification isn't for life. To stay certified, an armorer has to re-qualify every two years.

Glock advertising claims that its pistols are for the 21st Century. With many other manufacturers this might be dismissed as so much marketing hoopla; given the future-looking design features like injection molding and a minimizing of parts through careful design work, it seems likely that in Glock's case this isn't so. It is entirely likely that the Glock family of pistols will be one of the major players in at least the first few decades of the 21st Century.

Although overshadowed by the company's pistols, Glock bayonets and fighting knives continue to be used by soldiers around the world. (Photo courtesy of Glock, Inc.)

Glock's folding shovel continues to be manufactured and is quite possibly the best tool of its kind. (Photo courtesy of Glock, Inc.)

Chapter 2

Glock Variants

Glock has created a number of distinct versions of its original Glock 17 pistol. Most of these are created by reducing the length of the slide/barrel and grip assemblies, or by chambering the pistols for another cartridge.

In general the size changes occur within each distinctive chambering so that there is a standard sized model and a "chopped" or "hide-away" model suitable for use by detectives or others needing a compact pistol. Interestingly the smaller versions of the Glock generally only lose around 20 feet per second in muzzle velocity over their larger sister guns. And the shorter barrels often yield higher muzzle velocities than other manufacturers' full-sized pistols having the traditional lands and grooves which cause some loss in power as the bullet travels down the bore of the gun.

Other spin-offs of the original Glock 17 include the "L" or long-slide models, commemorative models, and selective-fire versions. To date, most of these have appeared only in the 9mm family of Glocks, with an "L" version chambered in .40 S&W having been introduced as the "Glock 23" (apparently with a nod toward U. S. civilians where such firearms have become popular with contest shooters).

Glock long-slide contest models have a strong showing in most pistol contests, though it is interesting to note that many contestants fire *standard* models of the Glock pistols—often scoring well in the process. This appears to reflect the fact that recently made Glocks are quite accurate right from the box; few other manufacturers can make such a boast.

The models listed in this chapter aren't the only variations of the Glocks that will be seen. Aftermarket accessories along with custom modifications and finishes make up variations that almost defy classification. That said, the many accessories or custom modifications that might be employed to create non-factory variants of the Glock pistols will be covered later in this book, with this chapter devoted solely to the official Glock models.

Most of the Glock models come in the company's "military issue" plastic case. This should include a spare magazine, a magazine loader, cleaning rod, brush, owner's manual, and the

Glock 19 pistol in its "issue" case including spare magazine, magazine loader, cleaning rod, brush, and owner's manual.

plastic case itself (which is even lockable for those with children in a home). This situation can vary, somewhat, however according to the specifications of the buyer. And probably not a few guns have the spare magazine "pilfered" by dealers interested in selling them to the customer for an additional price.

Even the pistol magazines display the innovative attitude of Gaston Glock's engineering skills. Not only do the magazines have "witness holes" on their rear sides which permit seeing how many cartridges are in them, the holes are also numbered. Shooters can see at a glance exactly how many rounds are left in a magazine.

Iron sights are generally standard with civilian and police Glocks. Military and some police buyers opt for optional self-luminous night sights for their "standard" gun. Both standard and night sights are available from Glock according to the ordering specifications; and many Glocks in the used gun market will be seen with aftermarket sights of one type or another.

Glocks manufactured before November 1991 could, in rare circumstances, have their firing pins lock in place. When this occurred, it caused the gun to fire when a round was being chambered, even creating burst firing or full auto discharges once in a great while. These pistols were recalled and upgraded with newly designed firing pins, firing pin safeties, and extractors. Pistols made after this date have the more reliable parts in them and don't suffer from these problems.

It's important to note that the old parts and new second generation parts can't be mixed. When new parts are placed in a gun, the old parts should be discarded, otherwise problems are likely to develop if an old part is inadvertently inserted into the firearm.

These newer "second generation" pistols are easily recognized by their deep serrations in the front of the grip strap, down the rear of the grip (from left to right on the lower section and up and down where the web of the hand touches the grip), and on the front of the trigger guard. Older guns had a "sandpaper" texture that ran around the grip and across the front of the trigger guard.

First generation Glocks can also be recognized by their serial number prefixes. Glocks will have a prefix that falls in the "AA" through "WF" range; Glock 19s, "AA" through "WJ"; Glock 20s, "AA" through "WW"; Glock 21s, "AA" though "XL"; Glock 22s, "AA" through "YA"; and Glock 23s, "AA" through "SK".

Internally, many parts in the Glock pistol have also undergone slight changes throughout the course of both generations. The most noticeable change has been the switch in making the recoil spring from metal rather than polymer, as was the case with early pistols. Later in 1991, the spring was made part of the guide by permanently securing it with a washer.

The original Austrian military specifications for the pistol it would adopt required that loaded magazines *not* drop from a pistol. To accommodate this requirement, Gaston Glock designed the polymer plastic magazine so it expands slightly when cartridges are in it and the spring under tension; original Glock 17 magazines work just the way the Austrian military leaders wanted them to. The magazines won't drop from the magazine well of the pistol when the magazine release button is depressed if there is any ammunition still in the magazine.

In actual combat, both because of the large capacity of the magazine as well as the tendency of shooters in combat to fire until they've exhausted all the rounds in their firearm, such a design requirement for magazines makes perfect sense. When the shooter of a Glock pistol realizes the gun is empty , the magazine will simply drop out when released, making a quick reload a cinch.

If a shooter exchanges a partially empty magazine for a full one during combat, it's good advice not to discard a partially full magazine for a full one. He might, after all, be hurting for ammunition in a short time and having a magazine with just a few cartridges in it could be a life saver. And, thanks to Austrian military specifications, the original-style Glock magazine makes it possible to exchange magazines without discarding the partially expended one in the gun since it won't drop out of the firearm. This allows exchanging the magazines and then pocketing the partially full one that has been replaced.

Of course competition shooters don't operate under such constraints. During contests, a quick exchange of magazines can give a shooter an edge.

As might be expected, those using a Glock pistol for competition shooting developed several methods of making the empty magazine drop from their firearms. Gunsmiths specializing in Glock work have created a magazine well insert that heats up and expands the grip. This resulting slightly greater inside dimension permits a magazine to fall freely from the gun when released.

The second solution employs aftermarket metal magazines coupled with a metal magazine release. Since the metal magazines don't expand when full, they drop cleanly from unaltered Glock grips. The only caveat here is a metal replacement magazine release must be used in conjunction with metal magazines. Otherwise the sharp metal edges of the magazine will cut into the magazine release lever, eventually ruining it.

Finally Glock, Inc., has created a solution for customers not wanting to take radical steps to make sure the magazine would fall from their pistols. Special order "free drop" magazines can be purchased from the company. Dimensioned slightly smaller than the standard magazine, these still hold the same number of cartridges. And drop free even if partially loaded.

The number of rounds a Glock 17 magazine holds is nothing short of confusing for many buyers. The original Glock 17 magazine design holds 17 rounds. But Glock engineers discovered that the addition of an extended floor plate could jack the number up by 2 without problem; the magazine with a floor plate holds to 19.

Soon Glock was selling this floor plate as the "Plus 2" option. That means that the original 17-round magazines can quickly become 19-round with the addition of the extended plate; Glock currently offers both magazines as standard for 9mm, .40 S&W, .45 ACP, and 10mm models making them capable of holding two more rounds when the base is added to the original magazine designed for them.

The Glock 18 is the machine pistol version of the Glock 17. When Glock engineers first experimented with the automatic pistol, it displayed the ability to go through a magazine of ammunition almost before the shooter could acquire his target. Consequently extended 9mm magazines were quickly created for the weapon. Originally both a 25- and 30-round magazine appears to have been created for the gun (and some early company literature even lists the 25-round magazine as an option).

In the end the 30-round magazine was selected and the 25-round magazine discarded. Then it was discovered that the 30-round magazine could actually hold 31 rounds and still function properly. Adding to the confusion, a Plus 2 magazine base placed on it created a 33-round capacity. And 33 rounds is the configuration it has kept since then. (Glock policy dictates that the 33-round magazine be sold only to qualified police and military buyers.)

Glock also produces "training" magazines for use with beginning shooters in the military or at police training schools. The magazine is colored a bright orange so it is readily recognizable both in and out of a pistol. The magazine *is* also fully functional and will accept ammunition.

What's the reason for an orange magazine that's fully functional?

It's designed to keep the training magazine from getting mixed up with duty magazines. Since a magazine being examined by beginning shooters is often dropped, jammed part way into a gun backwards, or other similar happenstances that can damage it, it may not function reliably. The orange color of training magazines keeps them from ever seeing duty outside the classroom.

Glock also makes a red polymer pistol frame that is assembled with a standard-colored slide and other parts. Unlike the training magazine, this training gun is nonfunctional and will not fire, making it ideal for use in classrooms with beginning shooters who often don't know how to treat a firearm and fail to understand that any gun should be kept pointed in a safe direction. When used in conjunction with the training magazine, the training pistol also makes it impossible to accidentally fire a gun, even if real rather than dummy rounds are placed in the magazine and chambered in the firearm.

To prevent its discharge, the firing pin hole on the red training pistol is welded shut. However, care should always be exercised to examine the breech face of a training pistol to ascertain that the firing pin hole is shut because a standard slide assembly can be placed on the training gun frame. While such a happenstance might be a one-in-a-million occurrence, care still should be exercised since a real slide on a training frame could fire a live round of ammunition.

Glock also offers a cutaway pistol for training purposes. This is a standard Glock 17 with milled cuts in various parts of its slide and frame to permit viewing the inner mechanism. The cuts in the barrel make it impossible for a round to be chambered and fired.

Other experimental, and working, models of firearms have also been created by Glock engineers. Among the guns known to have at least reached the proposal stage within the company are a single-column magazine pistol (which would be ideal for detectives or others needing a thin, concealed carry pistol) and a Glock carbine. To date most of these have been shelved and most likely won't go into production, despite the fact that more than a few Glock fans would like to own such firearms.

Regardless of the model, today's Glock pistols have been carefully engineered with parts that showed a tendency toward breakage quickly redesigned and made standard. This means all of the second-generation Glocks are, if possible, both durable and reliable than the original Glock 17. Breakage or jams are all but nonexistent.

Those with smaller hands will also appreciate the Glock's length of pull; unlike many modern "double-action" guns, the short pull of the Glocks are very accommodating to those with short fingers. Additionally, since the Glock has a single-piece molded grip, there are no grip panels or additional girth as with most other double-column magazine pistols; this, too, makes the Glock more suitable for shooters with smaller hands. (Oddly enough, those with large hands don't find the shorter pull of the trigger and the reduced circumference of the grip to be a problem and, in most cases, prefer the reduced size.)

Glock pistols chambered in 9mm and .40 S&W have the smallest grips and will most likely be the most comfortable for those with small hands. Glocks chambered in 10mm and .45 ACP have a noticeably thicker grip that may not be overly comfortable to smaller shooters.

The molded grip of the Glock pistols offers another safety plus. Often when semiautos are carried in holsters, the magazine release can be inadvertently depressed. This can lead to either the loss of the magazine altogether or will at least turn the firearm into a single-shot pistol since the cycling of the weapon will fail to chamber a new round. Such a happenstance is disastrous in combat and quite disconcerting in practice.

The molded grip of the Glock minimizes the possibility of this happenstance since the right side of the magazine release is even with the grip. That means a form-fitting holster tends to hold the off side of the release in place, making pressure on the release button unlikely to release the magazine. This, coupled with magazines that don't drop when the magazine contains cartridges, makes losing the magazine while the gun is holstered very unlikely. It should also be noted that most of the Glocks, thanks to their plastic frames, actually weigh less when loaded than many other companies' guns weigh empty. This makes the Glocks ideal for those who must carry a firearm all day long.

Traditionally lightweight guns have a downside: Recoil is more excessive since there is less mass to overcome during recoil. This is true with the Glock pistols, but not to as great an extent as one might imagine, thanks to the grip angle that tends to put the recoil force more in line with the barrel, a slight flex that takes place in the plastic frame itself, and a slide that is actually heavier than that of many other semiautos. Too, the high grip position in relation to the barrel makes the muzzle flip less noticeable with the Glocks because recoil has less leverage against the shooter's wrist; for many shooters this also reduces felt recoil. These factors cause many shooters to feel the recoil is no more extreme with a Glock than it is with a heavier pistol in the same chambering.

The light weight coupled with the slightly heavier trigger pull (as compared to some single-action guns) does make extremely good accuracy a bit harder to achieve without some practice. However even in this area the Glock seems to shine once the shooter becomes accustomed to it—as demonstrated by shooting contestants who have won trophies while firing a Glock.

Two types of plastic rear sights are currently found on pistols leaving Glock factories in the U. S. Both are "drift adjustable" by moving the sight in the channel cut in the top rear of the slide; this requires the use of the special tool Glock created for this purpose. If a drift punch is employed to move the rear sight, chances are it will damage the rear sight which is comprised of two sections, a plastic sight and a metal retainer. If the sight needs to be moved, then ideally a rear sight tool and some lubricant will be employed to make the work go smoothly. Otherwise the parts may part company, entailing some extra work and perhaps even the purchase of a new rear sight.

The standard Glock rear sight can't be adjusted for elevation while the "target" sight created to meet BATF requirements can, thanks to a small screw that will raise or lower the sight. The front sight consists of a front sight post having a single white dot in it; the rear sight notch is outlined in white. In addition to these two Glock-made sights, Glock also offers tritium insert glow-in-the-dark sights as an option.

Because the sights are plastic, many shooters feel they are a bit flimsy, though in actual use this doesn't prove correct. For those wanting steel sights, the best solution is to purchase a Glock with the optional "night sights." (The night sights are covered in the next chapter.)

The Glock rear sights come in five variants, the principal difference being in height. This permits changing the point of impact so the gun can be "zeroed" to the ammunition being used in it. These vary in height from 0.29-inches (high impact) to 0.24-inch (lowest impact). The adjustable sight is click adjustable from 0.20 to 0.29 inch giving it the ability to lower the point of impact a bit more than can be done by replacing a sight with its non-adjustable counterpart.

The Glock firing pin is designed for maximum strength. Its rectangular cross section ends in a convex nose that leaves primers with a distinctive indent. Shells fired in a Glock pistol are easily identified by the rectangular impression left in the primer by the firing pin hole of the breech with the firing pin indent itself in the center.

When it's all said and done, the Glock pistols are tough. Currently the specs for Glock guns call for them to fire at least 40,000 rounds of standard ammunition without part breakage or significant wear. This in itself is phenomenal, and there are even stories of Glock 17 pistols having 300,000 rounds fired through them without serious problem.

The ability to withstand such punishment is an important consideration, especially with police departments that have elected to use "+P+" ammunition, a very "hot" load that produces chamber pressures that border on the dangerous. Unlike some other manufacturers which recommend against firing +P+ 9mm cartridges, Glock has expressed no reservations about the use of these hot rounds and, in fact, even demonstrates firing the Glock 17 with these powerful rounds to show to potential buyers the strength of the pistol's design.

That said, +P+ cartridges aren't noted for the reliability in most pistols and the Glocks are no exceptions; and the tradeoff in reliability doesn't give all that much greater power. For those wanting more energy than the standard 9mm Luger cartridge offers, the best solution is to change to a more powerful cartridge like the .40 S&W or 10mm Auto. As noted below, Glock makes models in these chamberings. And these cartridges offer both reliability and power, without putting any extra strain on the firearm.

Glock 17

This is the model that, as they say, started it all. The original design has changed somewhat with the addition of grooves molded into the front and back strap of the pistol grip to secure it in wet conditions. Otherwise the gun has departed very little from its original design, though small dimensional changes have occurred over the course of its manufacture to beef up

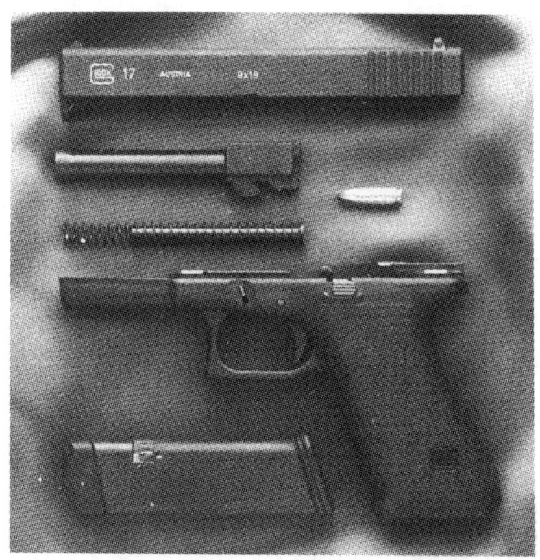

Disassembled first generation Glock 17, easily recognized by its "sandpaper" grip surface. (Photo courtesy of Glock, Inc.)

parts that proved prone to extra wear or breakage (minor concerns, it would appear, given the torture tests these guns seem to pass without problem during military tests).

Due to the use of interchangeable parts and computerized manufacturing, early Glock 17 pistols didn't have the tight fit found in many other of today's semiauto pistols. This is a plus in terms of reliability and parts replacement. But it is slightly detrimental to accuracy when comparing the gun to more expensive (and hand fitted) guns like the SIG Sauer lineup or the H&K P7.

Newer Glock 17s display greater accuracy, with many being nearly or as accurate as the Glock 17L (albeit with greater muzzle rise). However, for those who are really intent on target-grade accuracy, the solution is quite simple: Purchase the target model of the Glock 17, the Glock 17L, listed next. (To the joy of many Glock fans, it's often possible to purchase a Glock 17 for "carry" and a Glock 17L for target work for *less*

Second generation Glock 17 (Photo courtesy of Glock, Inc.)

than the cost of one of the more expensive hand-fitted pistols like the P7 or SIG Sauer 226.)

The NATO stock number for the Glock 17 is 1005-25-133-6775. Additionally most militaries designate the pistol with other stock numbers to accommodate it to their own systems.

Specifications for the Glock 17

Caliber: 9mm x 19 Parabellum (Luger)
Overall length of slide: 7.32 inches
Height: 5.43 inches
Width: 1.18 inches
Length between sights: 6.49 inches
Barrel length: 4.49 inches
Barrel rifling: Hexagonal profile with right hand twist
Twist rate: 1 turn per 9.84 inches
Standard magazine capacity: 17 rounds
Extended magazine(s): 19 and 33 rounds
Weight without magazine: 22.04 ounces
Weight of empty magazine: 2.75 ounces
Weight of full standard magazine: 9.87 ounces

Glock "Desert Storm"

This commemorative version of the Glock 17 memorializes Operation Desert Storm (which took place from January 16-February 27, 1991). Although no Glocks were *officially* issued by any of the governments involved in the operation, some soldiers, including U. S. officers, carried their own personal guns including Glock 17s. This was especially true with American pilots who were still armed with .38 Special revolvers left over from the Vietnam era. After getting approval from squadron commanders, many of these fliers purchased Glock pistols to carry with them on flights. Therefore Glock, Inc., felt justified in producing this version of its pistol, even though it wasn't the "official" sidearm of U. S. forces.

Only 1,000 of the Desert Storm commemorative pistols were produced. The top of the slide has a list of the 30 countries involved in the coalition engraved on it. The right side of the slide has "Operation Desert Storm" and "January 16-February

Ad for the Glock 17 "Desert Storm" commemorative pistol. (Photo courtesy of Glock, Inc.)

27, 1991" engraved on it while the left side of the slide reads: "New World Order Commemorative."

Except for the engraving, the Desert Storm version is otherwise identical to the standard Glock 17 both in finish and chambering. While this pistol is perfectly capable of being fired, the collector's value becomes less if the gun has been used. Therefore those owning one of these firearms are best advised to leave it in the box, removing it only to admire and clean from time to time.

Specifications for the Glock "Desert Storm"

Caliber: 9mm x 19 Parabellum (Luger)
Overall length of slide: 7.32 inches
Height: 5.43 inches
Width: 1.18 inches
Length between sights: 6.49 inches
Barrel length: 4.49 inches
Barrel rifling: Hexagonal profile with right hand twist
Twist rate: 1 turn per 9.84 inches
Standard magazine capacity: 17 rounds
Weight without magazine: 22.04 ounces
Weight of empty magazine: 2.75 ounces
Weight of full standard magazine: 9.87 ounces

Glock 17 "Thumb Safety"

Glock occasionally gets calls for a version of its pistol with a thumb-operated manual safety. In 1989, apparently to aid in the evaluation of such a pistol, the company created a prototype of its Glock 17 with a frame-mounted lever safety on the left side of the gun.

This prototype is otherwise identical to the standard Glock 17. Interestingly enough, when potential purchasers evaluate the standard gun against the thumb-safety prototype, they invariably choose the standard model. It therefore seems doubtful that the Thumb Safety version will ever go into production, though there's always a possibility, especially given the bureaucratic tendency to create purposeless parts specifications for weapons.

Specifications for the Glock 17 "Thumb Safety"
Caliber: 9mm x 19 Parabellum (Luger)
Overall length of slide: 7.32 inches
Height: 5.43 inches
Width: 1.18 inches
Length between sights: 6.49 inches
Barrel length: 4.49 inches
Barrel rifling: Hexagonal profile with right hand twist
Twist rate: 1 turn per 9.84 inches
Standard magazine capacity: 17 rounds
Weight without magazine: 22.4 ounces
Weight of empty magazine: 2.75 ounces
Weight of full standard magazine: 9.87 ounces

Glock 17L

The Glock 17L is the target pistol version of the Glock 17. As such the frame and most parts of the gun are identical to the Glock 17 with the only notable differences being the longer barrel, longer slide, extended magazine release button, and lighter trigger spring coupled with careful fitting of parts at the factory to assure better-than-average accuracy of the gun. The Glock 17L was first marketed in 1989 with early guns displaying only the "sandpaper" finish on the grip; later models have the front and backstrap grooves found on other current variants of the Glock.

The upper front of the slide is cut away, forming an oblong hole above the barrel from behind the front side back about two and 1/2 inches. The barrel below this opening has three 0.110-inch ports cut in it (very early Glock 17Ls lacked porting but most barrels have it on the 9mm models of the target pistol). These three ports cause jets of gas to rise from the barrel as the bullet passes down the bore. This jet action counters muzzle rise somewhat to help keep the gun on target for a rapid second shot; as importantly, the porting reduces felt recoil, a consideration for those firing extensively at the range. The large cut in the top of the slide is bigger than necessary simply to port gas. In fact it would appear that the opening also serves to reduce the weight of the slide. This helps keep the pistol

Right view of Glock 17L (Photo courtesy of Glock, Inc.)

Left view of Glock 17L. Insert shows porting of Glock 24C barrel which is nearly identical to the porting on current models of the Glock 17L. (Photo courtesy of Glock, Inc.)

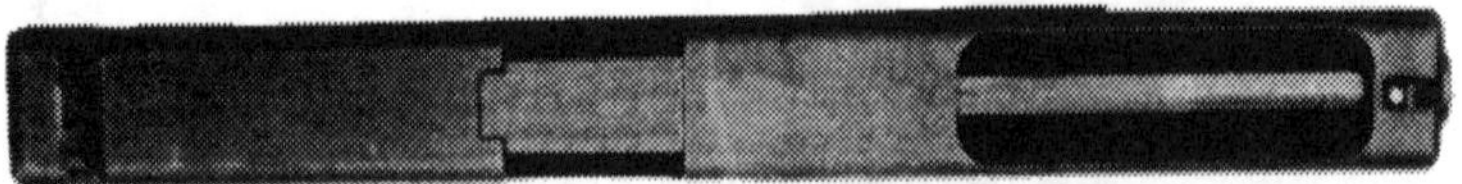

Top view of Glock 17L showing the slide cutout over the barrel.

cycling quickly for a second shot and also makes the lockup and other workings of the pistol similar to that of the Glock 17—no doubt a quick way to reduce the engineering needed to create the long slide version of the gun.

Usually a quality porting will also reduce the spread between shots, improving overall accuracy. This appears true with the Glock 17L porting since groups can be quite small with this pistol.

On the down side, most powders produce enough soot to blacken the front sight of the Glock 17L during extended firing. For most shooters this isn't much of a concern (and many may see it as an improvement if they dislike the white dot on the front sight). The soot is easily cleaned with standard powder residue solvents and gun cleaning fluids.

Because the large opening in the top of the slide is susceptible to the entrance of dirt or sand, the Glock 17L is obviously more susceptible to dirt than are its military versions. This isn't much of a concern to most users of this pistol, however, who will keep it meticulously clean since it will be employed as a target pistol.

Shortly after the introduction of the Glock 17L, Armando Valdes, a Miami, Florida police officer, won the 1990 World Shoot IX Championships at Adelaide, South Australia. And he used a stock Glock 17L (serial number DA-017U. S.) to win the competition. While much of the credit for such feats must

Armando Valdes displaying the world-class medals he won shooting his Glock 17L. (Photo courtesy of Glock, Inc.)

go to the skills displayed by the shooters, the fact that Valdes was able to win with a Glock 17L is not to be dismissed, either.

The Glock 17L displays more inherent accuracy than most shooters can make use of and also offers the muzzle control and recoil reduction needed for speed shooting. It's not surprising that the Glock 17L has become one of the most popular "minor caliber" contest guns in the IPSC (International Practical Shooting Confederation) contests.

Specifications for the Glock 17L

Caliber: 9mm x 19 Parabellum (Luger)
Overall length of slide: 8.85 inches
Height: 5.43 inches
Width: 1.18 inches
Length between sights: 8.07 inches
Barrel length: 6.02 inches
Barrel rifling: Hexagonal profile with right hand twist
Twist rate: 1 turn per 9.84 inches
Standard magazine capacity: 17 rounds
Extended magazines: 19 and 33 rounds
Weight without magazine: 23.63 ounces
Weight of empty magazine: 2.75 ounces
Weight of full standard magazine: 9.87 ounces

Glock 18 (First Generation)

The Glock 18 is the selective-fire version of the Glock 17. According to the scuttlebutt in the gun industry, this pistol was designed at the request of Austria's anti-terrorist "Cobra" team. Since the development of this specialized machine pistol, limited quantities have been sold with a few of the guns imported into the U. S. in 1989, most likely for consideration by anti-terrorist units in the American federal government.

As with other automatic weapons, when Glock 18s are test fired, they often build up a lot of heat. Glock company officials have a unique way of contending with this problem when demonstrating the Glock 18. They just dump the firearm into a bucket of water or run tap water over it. Because of the anti-

Early Glock 18 with ported barrel.

rust coating on all the metal parts, they can do this without fear of the gun corroding.

Although mechanically the Glock 18 is nearly identical to its semiauto sister guns (with an addition of a full-auto fire mechanism), key auto-fire parts are dimensionally different, including the slide, and trigger group. This prevents unauthorized creation of selective-fire guns, something that's always a worry to gun companies whose image can be tarnished by sales of such weapons to criminals and who may be open to lawsuits when amateur civilian gunsmiths or poorly supervised military armorers try creating a "special" pistol for their friends, only to have the experiment run amuck.

The most noticeable departure of the Glock 18's design from that of the original Glock 17 is the addition of a selective lever on the rear, left side of the slide. This lever has two positions; the upper is "semiauto" which makes the gun operate like a standard semiauto pistol. The lower position is marked with two dots and is the full-automatic position; the gun will continue to fire in this position until the release of the trigger or the magazine emptied.

Like other Glock pistols, the Glock 18 can have a variety of trigger pull weights by substitution of its spring. However ,the standard Glock 18 is issued with an 8-pound spring, most likely to minimize the chances of accidental discharge.

The current trend in machine pistols is to use a three-round burst mechanism. This is dictated by the muzzle climb such pistols demonstrate during full-auto fire; the first few bullets may strike the target but after that most of the projectiles will be headed skyward. The Glock 18 didn't go this route. Instead it is assumed that those using the gun will be trained to deliver short bursts or will be able to control the pistol.

Another departure from most other machine pistols is the lack of a detachable stock. The Glock 18 is designed to be fired more or less like a regular pistol and as far as anyone knows, a detachable stock was never created for the weapon. The automatic fire and lack of a stock dictate the need for a very, *very* skillful shooter if bullets aren't to become a dangerous spray when this gun is fired.

In an effort to counter some of the muzzle rise that occurs during automatic fire, early versions of the Glock 18s have a ported barrel that extends a half inch beyond the receiver. The three cuts in the barrel cause jets of hot gas to exit upward, pushing against the upward barrel flip of the gun.

Specifications for the Glock 18 (ported barrel version)

Caliber: 9mm x 19 Parabellum (Luger)
Overall length of slide: 7.78 inches
Height: 5.43 inches
Width: 1.18 inches
Length between sights: 6.49 inches
Barrel length: 5 inches
Barrel rifling: Hexagonal profile with right hand twist
Twist rate: 1 turn per 9.84 inches
Standard magazine capacity: 17 rounds
Extended magazines: 19 and 33 rounds
Weight without magazine: 22.5 ounces
Weight of empty magazine: 2.75 ounces
Weight of full standard magazine: 9.87 ounces

Glock 18 (second generation) with 33-round magazine created for it.

Glock 18 Second Generation

Although the porting of the first Glock 18 pistols was successful in muting muzzle climb, it also put enough pressure on the front sight during a string of automatic fire that the front sight was sometimes blown off the slide. Consequently newer, "second generation" guns have standard Glock 17 barrels lacking any sort of porting; these guns also have the standard grooves on the back and front of the grip and front of the trigger guard as found on second generation Glock 17s.

A person skilled in firing the Glock 18 can lay down an impressive amount of firepower in a short time, especially if he had several 33-round magazines available to him. Cyclic rate

Current production Glock 18 with 19-round magazine. Selector on the slide is set to the 2-dot, full auto position. (Photo courtesy of Glock, Inc.)

during auto fire will vary with the type of ammunition, but generally the Glock 18 will cook along at around 1,200 rounds per minute. That means a 33-round magazine will be empty in considerably less than a second if the shooter does more than barely tap the trigger. Little wonder, then, that those properly trained with the Glock 18 keep the selector in the semiauto position with the understanding that they will switch into full auto only when they find themselves in a tight jam.

Due to the clandestine nature of many potential buyers of the Glock 18, little is known about the actual numbers of these guns that have been purchased and issued. But the machine pistol has been seen in the hands of Italian airport police as well as Caribbean special police forces, suggesting that the Glock 18 might be "out there" in greater numbers than one might think.

Specifications for the Glock 18 (Second Generation version)

Caliber: 9mm x 19 Parabellum (Luger)
Overall length of slide: 7.28 inches
Height: 5.43 inches
Width: 1.18 inches
Length between sights: 6.49 inches
Barrel length: 4.49 inches
Barrel rifling: Hexagonal profile with right hand twist
Twist rate: 1 turn per 9.84 inches
Standard magazine capacity: 17 rounds
Extended magazines: 19 and 33 rounds
Weight without magazine: 21.91 ounces
Weight of empty magazine: 2.75 ounces
Weight of full standard magazine: 9.87 ounces

Glock 19

The Glock 19 is the short grip/short slide and barrel version of the Glock 17. As such the pistol can take both its smaller 15-round magazines as well as the larger 17-, 19-, and 33-round magazines created for the Glock 17 and Glock 18 (though the latter are generally issued only to qualified police and military

Relative sizes of the Glock 17 (top) Glock 17L (center) and Glock 19 (bottom). (Photo courtesy of Glock, Inc.)

Glock 19 pistol (Photo courtesy of Glock, Inc.)

buyers due to the ruckus created by the anti-gun legislators in Washington and elsewhere).

Despite the shorter dimensions of the Glock 19, most of its parts are identical to its sister pistol and interchangeable, making it an ideal addition to military and police users trying to keep some sense of commonality between various firearms, despite the different needs of plain-clothes detectives and officers contrasted against those needing a full-sized pistol. Because these pistols are apt to be used in "tense" situations by police and military purchasers, they are offered both with the standard 5-pound trigger spring as well as with the heavier 12-pound pull.

The Glock 19 was first marketed in 1988. NATO stock number for the Glock 19 is 1005-66-132-7731.

Specifications for the Glock 19

Caliber: 9mm x 19 Parabellum (Luger)
Overall length of slide: 6.85 inches
Height: 4.99 inches
Width: 1.18 inches
Length between sights: 5.98 inches
Barrel length: 4.02 inches
Barrel rifling: Hexagonal profile with right hand twist
Twist rate: 1 turn per 9.84 inches
Standard magazine capacity: 15 rounds
Extended magazines (Glock 17 & 18): 17, 19, and 33 rounds
Weight without magazine: 20.99 ounces
Weight of empty magazine: 2.46 ounces
Weight of full standard magazine: 8.99 ounces

Glock 19 "9x21mm"

The vast majority of Glock 19s made to date are chambered for the 9mm Luger. However, a very few have been manufactured by Glock in the 9x21mm cartridge that can be owned and used by civilians in many European countries that have outlawed "military" cartridges like the 9mm Luger. And it seems likely than even more may have been created by gunsmiths since simply rechambering a 9mm Luger barrel to the 9x21mm size is all that's needed to make the firearm compatible with the round.

The 9x21mm is simply a 9mm Luger that has its case lengthened by three millimeters to satisfy bureaucratic restrictions. The bullet in the 9x21mm is set lower than in the 9mm Luger so both cartridges have the same overall length. However, by using a hollow-point bullet and not seating it so far into the 9x21mm cartridge, the round can be loaded to fire bullets with greater velocity than can be safely achieved in the 9mm Luger. This, in theory at least, gives the 9x21mm the potential to come close to the .357 Magnum cartridge or the .40 S&W in its capabilities.

The Glock-manufactured guns produced in 9x21mm were apparently sold to U. S. investigators operating in Italy and elsewhere in Europe. The exact numbers of these guns that are in use remains unknown, but probably amounts to fewer than a dozen at the time of this writing.

The only difference between the Glock 19 9x21mm and standard Glock 19s in 9mm Luger will be the slightly larger chamber and "9x21mm" marking on the slide. Magazines and all other parts are identical on these guns since the two cartridges are basically identical.

Specifications for the Glock 19

Caliber: 9x21mm
Overall length of slide: 6.85 inches
Height: 4.99 inches
Width: 1.18 inches
Length between sights: 5.98 inches
Barrel length: 4.02 inches
Barrel rifling: Hexagonal profile with right hand twist
Twist rate: 1 turn per 9.84 inches
Standard magazine capacity: 15 rounds
Extended magazines (Glock 17 & 18): 17, 19, and 33 rounds
Weight without magazine: 20.99 ounces
Weight of empty magazine: 2.46 ounces
Weight of full standard magazine: 8.99 ounces

Glock "19L"

This "variant" isn't really a Glock catalog item. But often the work is done so well that it's hard to tell the modified pistol didn't come the way it is off the Glock assembly line. The pistol has the long slide of the Glock 17 but appears to have the frame of a Glock 19, giving it a compact "long slide" appearance (and, hence, the "L" tongue-in-cheek designation).

The pistol is actually a "chopped" Glock 17. And the modification makes a lot of sense for those needing a hideout pistol since — for most people — what makes a hide-out gun hard to conceal is the length of its grip, not of a gun's slide.

The plastic grip of the Glock makes the transformation rather simple, though great care has to be exercised in order not to ruin the pistol during the operation. The transformation is best done with a Model 19 to serve as a guide. This is laid on top of a Glock 17 and the length of the 19 grip scribed across the grip of the 17.

Next, a sharp X-acto blade or similar tool is used to carefully trim away the excess plastic nearly to the line. From that point on, sandpaper or (for the more adventurous) a Dremel tool is employed to remove the last of the plastic with the gunsmith carefully checking the length with a Model 19 short magazine. Once the magazine latches, the grip has been cut to the right length. And a new "Glock 19L" is created from a full-size Glock 17.

Of course this same technique might be employed to create a variety of other "variants" on the models listed in this chapter. To save space, the reader can use his imagination in regard to the variety of such custom pistols that is possible.

Glock 20

During the late 1980s, the U. S. FBI and other government agencies went on a search for a round that would be more effective than the 9mm Luger which had "failed" at least from a tactical standpoint in several gun battles. U. S. manufacturers were quick to comply with both pistols and ammunition to meet the perceived need for a more powerful round. After much

Glock 20, chambered for 10mm Auto. (Photo courtesy of Glock, Inc.)

evaluation and expense, in December, 1989, the FBI finally settled on the 10mm Auto.

The 10mm Auto in its original loading is a very hot round. It propels a 175-grain bullet from the barrel at 1,290 fps and produces 649 foot pounds of energy—almost twice as much as most 9mm Luger bullets. This makes the cartridge the rough ballistic equivalent of the .41 Magnum revolver load.

With the selection of the 10mm Auto cartridge, the FBI called for interested manufacturers to produce 10mm pistols and submachine guns for possible adoption by the agency. Since police departments as well as many civilians embrace the same ammunition and guns that the FBI does, manufacturers were quickly scrambling to produce both the 10mm cartridge as well as firearms chambered for it.

When the dust cleared, the FBI selected the Smith & Wesson 1076 as its issue 10mm pistol and the Heckler & Koch MP5/10 as its submachine gun. Unfortunately the switch over to the more powerful round hadn't been well thought out and the selection of guns proved premature. Because while the cartridge produced a massive amount of power that looked great on paper, in the field the FBI discovered that many of its agents weren't able to handle the added recoil produced by the ammunition.

Rather than admit an expensive mistake and start over, the FBI called for manufacturers to produce reduced-power 10mm cartridges; this caused the round to be bigger than it should have been for the amount of power it produced. Critics of the agency soon dubbed the reduced cartridge the "FBI Lite" and hinted that most agents couldn't handle a "real handgun." Adding to the insults was the fact that the reduced 10mm cartridges was the ballistic equivalent of the .45 ACP, a round the agency had rejected back in the 1930s.

When a quick check of the ballistics of the "FBI Load" is made, one also discovers that the 9mm Luger cartridge the 10mm was to replace actually offers *more* energy than the final, reduced FBI 10mm cartridge does. The FBI 10mm reduced load with its 180-grain bullet produces 361 foot pounds while the

Winchester 115-grain "Silvertip" that it was to replace produces 383 foot pounds.

So after all the bureaucratic shuffling, the FBI ended up with a cartridge slightly more "anemic" than the one the agency had set out to replace. Little wonder then that the agency quietly retired its new guns and reissued its S&W .357 revolvers to older agents and SIG Model 226s, chambered for the 9mm Luger (the cartridge the agency had set out to replace), to newer agents.

During the race to get a super-round, many manufacturers produced 10mm Autos including Glock. The Glock 20 is chambered for the powerhouse cartridge, apparently in an effort to win the original FBI contract being offered for a 10mm gun. Unfortunately no agencies were around to buy the gun when the cartridge fell out of the FBI's bureaucratic favor, and all interest in the round and pistols chambered for it was quickly evaporated.

That doesn't mean the round or Glock 20 are useless, though. Because while most shooters find the recoil of the full-power 10mm more than they wish to handle, some seasoned handgunners aren't recoil shy. These people feel the 10mm offers a lot of potential, especially when loaded with lighter bullets (which produce a lot of energy with lower recoil) which are topped over the original hot load designed for the cartridge. Perhaps to reach this market niche, Glock has continued to sell limited numbers of the model 20 which it introduced to the general shooting community in 1990 (after halting development work for a short time to create the company's new .40 S&W models of the pistol).

Because of the power of the 10mm when loaded to its full capacity, care does have to be exercised with it, especially if these cartridges are employed in self defense. There's a great likelihood that bullets will penetrate targets, making a potentially dangerous situation for innocent bystanders.

Specifications for the Glock 20

Caliber: 10mm Auto
Overall length of slide: 7.59 inches
Height: 5.47 inches

Width: 1.27 inches
Length between sights: 6.77 inches
Barrel length: 4.60 inches
Barrel rifling: Hexagonal profile with right hand twist
Twist rate: 1 turn per 9.84 inches
Standard magazine capacity: 15 rounds
Plus 2 optional magazine: 17 rounds
Weight without magazine: 27.68 ounces
Weight of empty magazine: 2.64 ounces
Weight of full standard magazine: 11.92 ounces

Glock 20L

In the early 1990s there was some talk at Glock, Inc., about a 6-inch barreled version of the Glock 20 which would be configured like the Glock 17L but chambered for the 10mm Auto round. Unfortunately the plans were coming together during the loss of interest in this cartridge by both the shooting public as well as the American law enforcement community. Consequently no commercial versions of this gun were ever marketed.

It's always possible that a gunsmith might cobble together a "Glock 20L" using Glock 17L or Glock 24 slide coupled with an extended or custom made barrel and spring assembly. But the chances of a genuine Glock version of this gun in 10mm seem slim at this time.

Should a Glock 20L ever come onto the market, it would make a dandy target pistol and would have the power to take medium-sized game at short ranges. As such it might arguably be an ideal survival gun for pilots or others needing a compact pistol with the capabilities of a carbine.

Glock 21

Introduced in 1991 and chambered for the .45 ACP, the Glock 21 is a sister gun to the Glock 20 with the principal differences between the two being their chamberings. While one might wonder if there is any market for another gun chambered for .45 ACP, the old cartridge does have a few things going for it. Most importantly, it has been proven over time and can be effective in combat as well as on the target range with suitable

Glock 21, chambered for .45 ACP. (Photo courtesy of Glock, Inc.)

loading. Furthermore, because the bullet leaving most .45 ACP cartridges travels at subsonic speeds, it is one of the few cartridges listed in this chapter that can be employed in a practical manner with a silencer—an important consideration with some military buyers.

When compared to most other .45 ACP guns, the Glock 21 has a lot going for it. Most notably is the high capacity magazine that holds 13 rounds, thanks to its double-column design (giving it almost twice the capacity of most single-column pistols chambered for this round). Additionally the lack of safety to fool with, consistent pull from the first to last shot, and other features that most people find attractive with the other Glock pistols apply to the Glock 21 as well. For these reasons the Glock 21 would seem to have a better chance than most other .45 pistols when it comes to survival in the marketplace, with the possibly exception of the time-honored 1911 design that has taken on a following that borders on fanaticism.

It's interesting to note that the magazine catch on the Glock 21 (and Glock 20) is actually the extended catch created for the Glock 17L. It seems that the extra high "fast reloading" 17L catch was perfect for the wider frame of the Glock 21 and 20;

Glock engineers utilized it in the guns, thereby doing away with the need to create a new, expensive molding to make a third style of catch.

For shooters wanting a modern gun chambered for the .45 ACP, the Glock 21 is a good bet.

Specifications for the Glock 21

Caliber: .45 ACP
Overall length of slide: 7.59 inches
Height: 5.47 inches
Width: 1.27 inches
Length between sights: 6.77 inches
Barrel length: 4.60 inches
Barrel rifling: Hexagonal profile with right hand twist
Twist rate: 1 turn per 15.75 inches
Standard magazine capacity: 13 rounds
Plus 2 optional magazine: 15 rounds
Weight without magazine: 25.22 ounces
Weight of empty magazine: 3.1 ounces
Weight of full standard magazine: 11.78 ounces

Glock 22

The Glock 22 is another spin-off from the Glock 17 with the principal difference being its chambering for the more powerful .40 S&W. The newer cartridge has proven to be more and more popular in the U. S. with a variety of shooters. Both contest shooters and reloaders like the .40 S&W because its greater power makes it more flexible and capable of higher scoring and accuracy.

For much the same reason, many choosing a pistol for self defense have also opted for the .40 S&W since it boosts a bullet to nearly the same specifications of the .357 Magnum, a cartridge that has proven to be one of the best among the various pistol rounds when it comes to terms of actually stopping an attacker.

The Glock 22 was introduced to the marketplace in 1990, thanks to some quick thinking on the part of Gaston Glock.

The Glock 22 "leap frogged" models 20 and 21 in order to get the new pistol, chambered for the potent .40 S&W, onto the marketplace. (Photo courtesy of Glock, Inc.)

Right view of Glock 22 (Photo courtesy of Glock, Inc.)

In January of 1990, the inventor visited the SHOT Show in Las Vegas to display prototypes of his .45 ACP and 10mm Glocks. While at the show, he obtained the ballistic data for the new .40 caliber semiauto pistol cartridge that Smith & Wesson had developed in conjunction with several ammunition manufacturers.

Glock quickly recognized the potential of this new cartridge and a month later instructed his engineers to drop their work on production of the 10mm and .45 ACP models of his pistols and instead had them concentrate on producing a new Glock model chambered for the .40 S&W cartridge.

By April 1990, Glock had his first prototypes in .40 S&W and quickly sent them to various U. S. Agencies for testing. A month later the feedback from the testers was used to finalize the new gun's specifications and the Glock 22 (and its compact Glock 23 sister pistol) were being offered for sale, a record production of a new pistol if ever there was one.

By August, 1990, just eight months after Gaston Glock had heard of the new .40 S&W cartridge, the South Carolina Law Enforcement Division was receiving its first shipment of the new pistols. By September of that year 33 law enforcement agencies had either ordered or received Glock pistols chambered for the .40 S&W.

Unfortunately the story doesn't end there. During the testing of the prototype pistols, the California Highway Patrol, for reasons known only to those involved in its trials to adopt a new .40 S&W pistol, placed two Glock prototypes alongside other companies' guns for torture testing, despite the fact that Glock company officials had taken pains to tell the patrol that the samples were only for evaluation, not for testing.

Not surprisingly the slide and some minor parts cracked during the tests and the slides failed to lock open after the last shot since the magazines in the guns were simply modified 9mm magazines from Glock 17s. The California Highway Patrol recorded all of these shortcomings as failures and then circulated the results, for a short time giving the new Glock 22 pistol an undeserved black eye among potential buyers.

Fortunately off-the-assembly-line Glock 22s were soon available for testing by other agencies. And these production guns proved to be as durable as their 9mm sisters. Today the Glock 22 has the same good reputation that its sister pistols enjoy.

Specifications for the Glock 22

Caliber: .40 S&W
Overall length of slide: 7.32 inches
Height: 5.43 inches
Width: 1.18 inches
Length between sights: 6.49 inches
Barrel length: 4.49 inches
Barrel rifling: Hexagonal profile with right hand twist
Twist rate: 1 turn per 9.84 inches
Standard magazine capacity: 15 rounds
Plus 2 optional magazine: 17 rounds
Weight without magazine: 22.92 ounces
Weight of empty magazine: 2.75 ounces
Weight of full standard magazine: 11.46 ounces

Glock 23

The Glock 23 is the "hide out" version of the Glock 22, having a shorter barrel/slide assembly and shorter grip than is found on the larger gun. The Glock 23 was introduced in 1990 and, in addition to its shorter magazine, will also accept the longer magazine designed for the Glock 22.

Specifications for the Glock 23

Caliber: .40 S&W
Overall length of slide: 6.85 inches
Height: 4.99 inches
Width: 1.18 inches
Length between sights: 5.98 inches
Barrel length: 4.02 inches
Barrel rifling: Hexagonal profile with right hand twist
Twist rate: 1 turn per 9.84 inches
Standard magazine capacity: 13 rounds
Extended magazines (Glock 22): 15 and 17 rounds

Glock 23 (Photo courtesy of Glock, Inc.)

Weight without magazine: 21.16 ounces
Weight of empty magazine: 2.46 ounces
Weight of full standard magazine: 9.87 ounces

Glock 24

Introduced in 1994, the Glock 24 is the .40 S&W version of the Glock 17L target pistol. Like the 17L, the frame and most parts of the Glock 24 are identical to the standard-sized Glock 22 with the only notable differences being the longer barrel, longer slide, and lighter (4.5-pound) trigger spring coupled with careful fitting of parts at the factory to assure better-than-average accuracy of the gun. "Drop free" magazines that don't stay in the well when cartridges are in them come as standard parts with the Glock 24 since these magazines are the best for contest shooters.

The Glock 24 has an open section on the top of its slide but no porting, perhaps in an effort to avoid the "blackened sight" that plagues the Glock 17L as well as to make it "legitimate" for some types of shooting contests. For those interested in a ported barrel, the Glock 24C has ports but is otherwise identical to the Glock 24.

Specifications for the Glock 24

Caliber: .40 S&W
Overall length of slide: 8.85 inches
Height: 5.43 inches
Width: 1.18 inches
Length between sights: 8.07 inches
Barrel length: 6.02 inches
Barrel rifling: Hexagonal profile with right hand twist
Twist rate: 1 turn per 9.84 inches
Standard magazine capacity: 15 rounds
Plus 2 optional magazine: 17 rounds
Weight without magazine: 26.45 ounces
Weight of empty magazine: 2.99 ounces
Weight of full standard magazine: 11.46 ounces

Glock 24C

The Glock 24C is identical to the Glock 24 but has a ported barrel. The porting is at the forward, top area of the barrel just below the open section at the top of the slide. Like its sister guns, the Glock 24C comes with a 4.5-pound trigger spring and designed for maximum accuracy.

Specifications for the Glock 24C

Caliber: .40 S&W
Overall length of slide: 8.85 inches
Height: 5.43 inches
Width: 1.18 inches
Length between sights: 8.07 inches
Barrel length: 6.02 inches
Barrel rifling: Hexagonal profile with right hand twist
Twist rate: 1 turn per 9.84 inches
Standard magazine capacity: 15 rounds
Plus 2 optional magazine: 17 rounds
Weight without magazine: 26.45 ounces
Weight of empty magazine: 2.99 ounces
Weight of full standard magazine: 11.46 ounces

Glock 25

The Glock 25 is simply a Glock 19 chambered for the .380 ACP cartridge. Although some have claimed this pistol was created for the European market, in fact company officials at Glock say it was created for Brazil civilian use (which ownership of pistols chambered for rounds as powerful as the 9mm Luger are not often permitted). Except for chambering and the modification of the recoil spring, magazine, and a few other parts, the Glock 25 is identical to the Glock 19.

Because BATF rules don't give any "points" for small pistols chambered for the .380, it appears that it is impossible for the Glock 25 to be imported into the U. S. as things now stand. This has to be one of the great oddities of current American law that prevents the importing of a pistol chambered for a less powerful cartridge because it is less "sporting" than a similar gun chambered for 9mm. There's no telling for bureaucratic insanity.

Specifications for the Glock 25
Caliber: .380 ACP
Overall length of slide: 6.85 inches
Height: 4.99 inches
Width: 1.18 inches
Length between sights: 5.98 inches
Barrel length: 4.02 inches
Barrel rifling: Hexagonal profile with right hand twist
Twist rate: 1 turn per 9.84 inches
Standard magazine capacity: 15 rounds
Weight without magazine: 20.99 ounces
Weight of empty magazine: 2.46 ounces

Glock 26

The Glock 26 surfaced late in 1995 with a few sales in the U. S. starting late in 1995. The pistol had a little trouble getting the approval of BATF; the federal agency insisted that the handgun had to be "sporterized" in order to be brought in. Consequently "target" grips with finger and thumb swells were molded into its grip and adjustable target sights mounted on its slide.

Chambered for the 9mm Luger cartridge, the Glock 26 feeds from a double-column magazine and is nearly three-fourths of an inch shorter both in length and height as compared to the Model 19. This makes it even more ideal for concealed carry, a purpose it will most likely serve well.

Specifications for the Glock 26
Caliber: 9mm x 19 Parabellum (Luger)
Overall length of slide: 6.1 inches
Height: 4.24 inches
Width : 1.18 inches
Length between sights: 5.23 inches
Barrel length: 3.46 inches

Barrel rifling: Hexagonal profile with right hand twist
Twist rate: 1 turn per 9.84 inches
Standard magazine capacity: 10 rounds
Extended magazines (Glock 19, 17, and 18): 15, 17, 19, and 33 rounds
Weight without magazine: 19 ounces
Weight of empty magazine: 2.16 ounces

Glock 27

The Glock 27 also was announced by Glock late in 1995 along with the 26; American sales started the first of 1996. Like it's 9mm counterpart, the .40 S&W Glock 27 was "sporterized" with "target" grips molded into the frame and adjustable target sights on the slide. The Glock 27 feeds from a double-column magazine and is nearly three-fourths of an inch shorter both in length and height as compared to the Model 19.

Specifications for the Glock 27

Caliber: .40 S&W
Overall length of slide: 6.1 inches
Height : 4.24 inches
Width: 1.18 inches
Length between sights: 5.23 inches
Barrel length: 3.46 inches
Barrel rifling: Hexagonal profile with right hand twist
Twist rate: 1 turn per 9.84 inches
Standard magazine capacity: 9 rounds
Weight without magazine: 19 ounces
Weight of empty magazine: 2.16 ounces

GLOCK®

Chapter 3

Aiming Systems

Although early Glock 17s weren't noted for their tack-driving accuracy, this has changed as more and more of the guns have been produced. Most Glock pistols have greater potential accuracy right out of the box than the owners of the firearm can take advantage of and most standard guns rival the accuracy of the company's long-slide target versions. Consequently, mounting quality sighting systems on one of these guns can make a lot of sense on a hunting or contest gun because it enables shooters to home in on targets a bit better and a bit faster. For those with some types of vision problems, a pistol-mounted scope can also give a clearer view of the target and sights.

Whether a shooter adds a laser sight, optical scope, or even a flashlight to his pistol, there are some tradeoffs, however, because a Glock pistol with any of these devices mounted on it is considerably more awkward a piece of equipment than without them. Where a Glock pistol is light and easy to carry, a scoped Glock is heavy and has an added appendage on its top, dictating either a custom or competition holster. The latter opens a whole new range of problems since scopes are relatively fragile compared to iron sights; one drop or glancing blow may put a scope out of kilter or even destroy it.

The extra bulk of a scope on a pistol dictates more weight to be carried and lifted to target, not minor considerations for those carrying the pistol around all day or doing a lot of shooting at the range. And finding a good holster for a scoped or "lasered" handgun can be tough (though, as we'll see in the next chapter, manufacturers are currently working to supply the needs of those needing holsters and other accessories to go with pistols having specialized aiming gear mounted on them either above the slide or below the front of the frame).

Arguably iron sights—or in the case of the Glocks—plastic sights are usually the best and cheapest solution to bringing a gun onto target for most shooters. Telescopic sighting systems can be fast if a shooter puts in practice with them; but slight movements of a shooter's hand and the relatively narrow fields of view presented by most scopes makes quickly finding a target less than ideal. Scopes, like iron sights, require a lot of practice before a shooter really becomes proficient with them.

For those who have shot and practiced with iron sights for many years, another problem occurs when scoping a Glock; the gun is habitually raised to bring the iron sights to eye level, dictating a second motion to lower the gun a tad to align the eye with the scope. Because of this latter complication, many seasoned shooters find it takes a lot of extra practice before they can overcome old habits to bring a pistol on target with a scope as fast as they can with iron sights. These factors can cause critical extra moments before the crosshairs get on target if a shooter is unfamiliar with the scope system. Shooters shouldn't depend on a scoped pistol in the field or for self defense until aiming it has become a reflex.

That said, some shooters because of eye problems or other reasons find iron sights almost impossible to use; these shooters will benefit from optical systems mounted on a pistol and are more than willing to put in the extra practice needed to rapidly acquire a target with a scope, since it is an all or nothing proposition for these people when it comes to pistol shooting.

This rambling preamble out of the way, here are a few of the sighting systems currently available for the Glock pistols.

Scopes and Scope Mounts

A scope doesn't turn a shooter into dead-eye Dick. A poor shooter with a scoped pistol will still be a poor shooter, scope or not. But if enough practice is put into aiming a scoped Glock pistol, it will start to show in terms of increased shooting skills.

One added plus with optical scopes is that the magnification makes identifying the target easier. Furthermore, competition shooters have demonstrated that once a scope finally is mastered and the habit of bringing its aiming point up in front

Glock "decked out" with a B-Square scope mount and B-Square laser sight and mount. This assembly is bulky and not for the average shooter; it does make it possible to quickly acquire a target in any lighting condition. (Photo courtesy of B-Square, Inc.)

of the eye perfected, an electric dot scope on a pistol can be much faster and more accurate than a gun having only iron sights, all other things being equal. So for those willing to put in the practice and put up with the extra weight and frailties of a scope, there are some important edges to be gained.

There are several good scope-mount systems available for mounting scopes to a Glock pistol. Once in place, the mounts provide a rock solid mount for the standard Weaver rings that will accommodate most scopes. Because the various models of the Glock are so similarly dimensioned, mounts designed for the Glock fit all current models of the pistol from the compact "hideout" models on up to the long-slide versions, in all of the calibers currently offered by Glock. B-Square offers a "blued" model (actually black-finished aluminum) which sells for $69.95 (product number 12702). The B-Square mounting system requires a very small amount of gunsmithing work since the gun

B-Square scope mount for Glock pistols. (Photo courtesy of B-Square, Inc.)

has to be partially disassembled to fasten the mount to the frame. The mount is then held securely in place by a pin that replaces the original Glock trigger pin along with the adjustment screws on the mount. (Should the shooter later want to remove the mount for some reason, the task is equally simple with a quick trip to the gunsmith).

A "Competition Mount" is also offered by B-Square for $120 (product number 12072). This unit requires a bit of gunsmithing to secure it to the frame of the Glock but also gives the gun a sleeker look since it is held in place by screws that connect into the frame of the firearm rather than clamping around the frame. For those planning to use their pistol in contest shooting, this would seem like the best option available, especially for long-slide target versions of the Glock.

Aimtech offers a mount that fits all models of the Glock; cost is $63.25. Finished in black, the mount can be installed in just minutes by the shooter without any gunsmithing work. Like the B-Square mounts, the Aimtech mount rides high enough to permit use of the pistol's iron sights if the scope should get damaged.

Once a shooter has a scope mount for his pistol, the next big decision is what type of scope to attach to it. Currently scopes fall into two broad categories, electric "dot" scopes and optical scopes.

Optical scopes with traditional crosshairs and no electronics to contend with have been on the scene a long time, though putting them onto a pistol has been a relatively modern occurrence. Most shooters find that 1-power magnification is generally best for handguns since it permits aiming with both eyes open, giving the illusion of a wider field of view since the shooters' eyes combine the two images coming into his brain. However some shooters, especially hunters, may want some magnification; in such a case, a 2x, 3x, or even 4x power scope might be a more suitable choice than a 1x-power scope.

Tasco's "Proclass" pistol scopes are good picks for handgunners wanting an optical scope. This line of scopes comes in a variety of powers and reticules. The scope's 30mm tubes give longer eye relief and a greater field of view. The scopes are sold with 30mm rings so mating them to standard-sized Weaver mounts is simple.

Tall shooters considering the purchase of a cross-hair optical scope should always check for adequate eye relief (the distance from the eye to the scope) before they make any purchases; a few optical cross-hair scopes don't have long enough eye relief for those with longer arms. Also, it's a good idea to purchase a name brand scope like Bushnell, Tasco, or others to insure quality of the optics as well as simplified repair of the scope if it is ever damaged. Bargain scopes with little-known names are almost always iffy at best and a waste of money when they go haywire.

Dot scopes place a dot at the center of a scope's field of view, dispensing with cross hairs and the like. That said, it would seem that this wouldn't be a big advantage; and it wasn't—until manufacturers started "lighting" the dot. Then it became very easy for a shooter to find the glowing dot in his field of vision and, with practice, permitted quick acquisition of a target. This changed the whole idea of scopes for many shooters and is the reason dot scopes are seen on many competition guns.

There are two types of dot scopes: Those operating on available light and those functioning with a small battery to produce a glowing dot via an LED (Light-Emitting Diode). Of the two, the battery-operated version has become the most popular since the brightness of the dot can be adjusted according to the tastes of the shooter.

Most competition shooters employ guns sporting electric "dot" scopes. The big advantage of this type of scope is that they permit aiming with both eyes open and have little if any parallax problems. They're just as tough as other optical scopes to bring onto the bull's eye, but shooters who practice extensively with these scopes can learn to rapidly acquire a target. If speed is a shooter's goal, then the dot scope coupled with lots of practice is a good bet.

Another big plus dot scopes have over cross-hair optical scopes is that they can be used in the dark, producing a sight picture much like that of the laser—without giving away the shooter's presence to anyone in the target area since a dot scope, unlike a laser sight (more on these in a bit), produces no indication of its presence to the front of the pistol. Dot scopes thus work not only during the day but at dusk or even nighttime for those using the firearm in self defense. This can be an important plus for many shooters.

Dot scopes also have unlimited eye relief and don't suffer from any parallax problems; this permits a target to be accurately hit without placing the dot in the center of the field of view in the scope picture, an important plus for quick target acquisition and shooting. Most dot scopes display a tiny (usually red but sometimes green) ball of light in the center of the scope "picture."

Electric scopes are quick in acquiring targets, but they aren't quick to turn on. It's generally necessary to twist a knob or, more rarely, throw a switch. Unfortunately, no enterprising manufacturer has yet marketed a pressure switch similar to those described below which are common to laser sights nor has anyone created a mercury switch that turns the scope on when the pistol is drawn from its holster. For this reason electric scopes should be turned on the moment a shooter expects to be shooting—an especially important point for those using these scopes for hunting or self defense. (Fortunately battery life is very long for these scopes, making it possible to leave the scope on for extended time without fear of running down the battery—provided the battery is replaced on a regular basis.)

Among the best electric dot scopes currently available are those offered by Aimpoint, AAL Optics, and Tasco. Tube size on the models offered by these companies varies; older 1-inch models are less expensive but give a narrower field of view than the newer 30mm or larger scopes do making them less rapid in acquiring the target. Most shooters will discover they can acquire a target more rapidly if they purchase one of these larger scopes for their handgun.

In addition to costing less, the 1-inch tube scopes are also more compact. For those trying to carry a scoped gun in a holster, it makes a lot of sense to go with a 1-inch scope simply because it is smaller and therefore less apt to be bumped or damaged when being carried.

The Aimpoint 5000 offers a 30mm field of view. This scope is available in black matte or stainless finish, the scope can be powered by a pair of mercury SP675 batteries or, for cold weather use, a single lithium 2L76 or DL1/3N battery. The scope is 5.5 inches long and weighs 5.8 ounces; cost is $320. Since the 5000 scopes have tubes too large for one-inch Weaver rings, these are included with the scope and will accommodate most Weaver-style mounts.

Aimpoint's "Comp" scope is designed to capture a share of the competition shooting market. The 30mm field of view helps a shooter lock onto his target. Weight of the Comp scope is 4.75 ounces and the length is 4.365 inches. The scope comes with rings to permit easy mounting on Weaver rails.

Tasco offers the "ProPoint" series of electric dot scopes with 30mm tubes (which give a 25mm field of view) or 40mm tubes (giving a 30mm field of view). These scopes come with mounting rings and detachable sun shields that screw onto the front and/or rear of the scope. The ProPoints come in three dot sizes (dot size is measured in minutes of angle with a minute covering a 1-inch area at 100 yards).

The Propoint PDP2 and PDP3 have 30mm tubes with a choice of 5- or 10-minute sized dots; the PDP2 has an on/off switch while the PDP3 has an 11 position rheostat for fine adjustment of dot brightness. The PDP4 has a 45mm tube and comes in three dot sizes of 10, 15, and 20 and has a 11-position detent. Costs vary according to models and the best deals offered by dealers, but the Propoint scopes generally sell in the $190 to $250 range.

AAL Optics offers a 30mm dot scope as their "Ultra Dot 30" which incorporates its battery pack into the small, click-adjustable brightness control knob, eliminating the cumbersome projecting battery pack seen on most other dot scope designs. The cost for the Ultra Dot 30 is $189; the scope is available in both stainless and matte black finishes.

The AAL dot scopes have always had the plus of being an ounce or so lighter than their competitors. Recently AAL has shaved off even more weight by switching to a tough injection molded composite tube (rather than aluminum) for the body of the "Ultra Dot Patriot" (the "Patriot" designation coming from the fact that it is one of the few dot scopes that's made entirely in the U. S. A). In addition to its light weight, this scope has a fiber optic system that makes its red dot sharper and rounder than the dot of some other scopes. Cost is also less; the scope retails for $119.

Recently several "tubeless" dot scopes have appeared on the market. These have the advantage of permitting the shooter to see the red dot on the mirrored lens at the front of the scope since it lacks a tube to block the view. This makes for quicker target acquisition and also a lighter sight. Of course the downside is that the sight is open making it somewhat more sensitive to dirt than a sealed scope system. For those using the scope for self defense, it should also be noted that the LED may be somewhat visible from the side on some of these units, a potential tactical problem in a very dark environment.

Oddly enough, the tubeless system is based on an early 1900s-vintage shotgun sight. This design was resurrected in the 1970s by Daisy Air Rifles as a cheap plastic scope for air guns. Later, this design was modified with the addition of an LED (Light-Emitting Diode) and small electric watch battery so it would work in all types of light rather than just bright sunlight.

Since the patent has expired on the original design, several manufacturers have created more expensive versions of the open sight with a larger lens and 1-inch Weaver mounts, rather than the smaller 7/8-inch mounts common to air rifles and .22 rifles. But except for the larger field of view and sealed battery packs, these more expensive open sights are quite similar to those created by Daisy.

Among the better of these "new" open tube sights designed for pistol mounting is the "C-More" which has proven to be popular with many competition shooters including IPSC World Champion (1993), Matt McLearn.

Currently Emerging Technology offers an open dot scope as its "Dualdot" model in its LaserAim series of products. In addition to providing an optical dot, this scope has a laser sight built into its base which can be ideal for some night shooting situations. Cost of the Dualdot is $225.

Whether you choose an electric dot scope or an optical scope, it's important to put in extensive practice with it. This makes it possible to quickly bring the pistol onto its intended target without having to "hunt" around for it.

Sights

For shooters with good eyesight, arguably the best sights for the Glock pistols are the ones the guns come with or replacement iron sights. These sights have been carefully designed, fit the guns perfectly, and are generally best suited to the tasks the gun will be employed for. And unlike laser, dot, or optical sights, they don't add a lot of bulk to the firearm. In addition to adjustable rear sights, Glock offers two variations of its fixed sights. These come in slightly different heights, permitting compensation for various types of ammunition

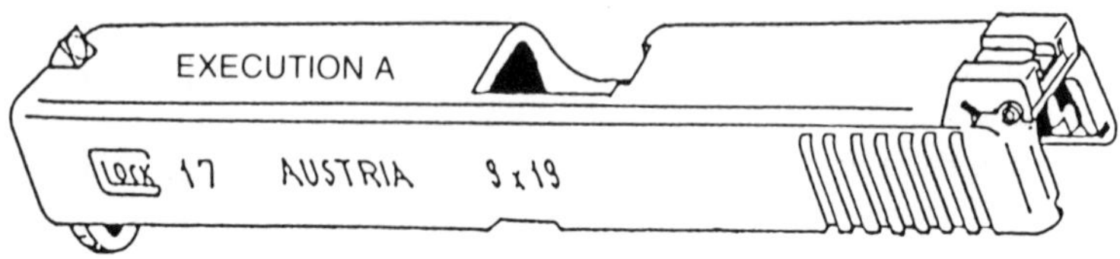

Slide with Glock's adjustable rear sight. (Drawing courtesy of Glock, Inc.)

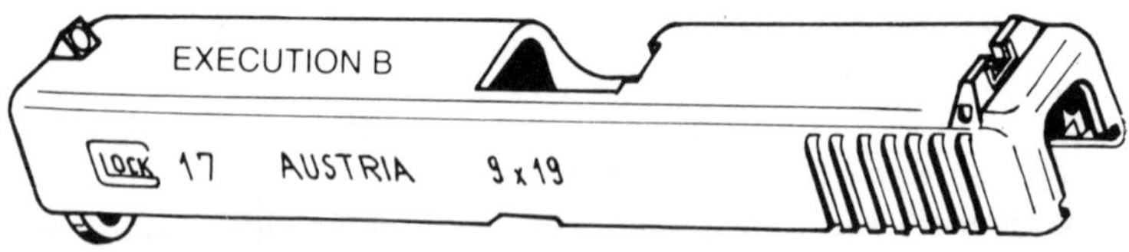

Slide showing standard "fixed" rear sight originally designed for the Glock pistols. (Drawing courtesy of Glock, Inc.)

which may have slightly different points of impact at longer ranges.

Front and/or rear replacement sights are easier to mount on a Glock if one of the company's sight tools is employed for the task. This tool is also useful for altering the windage (left/right point of aim) on the rear sight.

Since the majority of gunfights occur at night or in poorly lit areas, nightsights (iron sights with glow-in-the-dark inserts)

Glock's sight adjustment tool (K) shown with the company's fixed rear sights (I) in two heights to compensate for bullet drop with various types of ammunition and the compnay's night sights (J). (Photo courtesy of Glock, Inc.)

make a lot of sense. These sights assist in locating a target in dim light.

Most modern night sights contain small glass vials of tritium gas (an isotope of hydrogen); these tiny containers are inserted into small holes drilled in the front and on either side of the rear sight notch. Tritium sights give a bright glowing points of light that are easily aligned with a target in the darkest of environments. The life of the radioactive material is such that the dots will remain bright and useable at night for at least 10 years before they need to be replaced.

Of course radioactive things make most thinking people a bit squirmy. But tritium is very safe since no radiation other than visible light penetrates the glass vial containing the radioactive gas. And even if a vial of a tritium sight breaks indoors—an occurrence that is hard to imagine unless the sight were abused—the exposure to radiation is minimal since the gas quickly dissipates into the atmosphere (though to be on the safe side, the room should be aired out if such an accident chances to occur).

In addition to night sights, there is a huge variety of aftermarket iron sights available for the Glock pistols; probably the best source for these is Brownells, which has *all* of the sights listed below in stock (with the exception of the "Aro-Sights" which must be ordered directly from Aro-Tek). Brownells is just a phone call away for those with plastic charge cards.

The Heinie Specialty replacement sights are designed to give a very low-profile sight picture by taking advantage of the flat slide top of the Glock pistols (which helps some shooters bring their gun onto target more quickly). An added plus of these sights is that they ride lower making them slightly less apt to get hung up in a holster, clothing, or whatever. The front and rear sights also lack any dots or other "white" markings and do have serrated areas toward the shooter, producing a "black silhouette" sight picture preferred by some shooters. Cost is $43 from Brownells.

Millett offers adjustable rear sights for the Glock pistols; all require a companion front sight. The rear sights are adjustable both for elevation and windage with miniature screws located on the sight. The Millett rear sight blade is available in one of three choices including a target, white outline, or 2-dot configuration; cost is $55.60 for any of these three styles for any model of the Glock. The required front sights are available in white, orange, white dot, and black serrated styles for $16 each.

Millett also offers adjustable glow-in-the-dark tritium night sights for the Glocks. These cost $135 per set of front and rear sights. Like the standard Millett sights, the rear sight is adjustable for both windage and elevation.

Wayne Novak has created a "Carry" rear sight for the Glock guns. The sights are rounded to make them snag free and have a large, rebated sight notch for a clear picture of the target. Cost is $30 for a standard black rear sight; a two-white-dot sight costs $35. A plain front sight costs an additional $20 while a "dot" front sight costs $27.

Aro-Tek's rear "Aro-Sights" are available in three distinct styles including a glow-in-the-dark night sight, a two-dot sight, and a no-dot target version. Note the unique mounting system employing a bracket and two screws to hold the sight in place on the slide. (Photo courtesy of Aro-Tek, Inc.)

Aro-Tek's front sights include (left to right) the "Aro-Glow" glowing day sight, "Aro-Sights" target sight, the "Aro-Tek" night sight, and the "White Dot" model. (Photo courtesy of Aro-Tek, Inc.)

Pachmayr offers an adjustable rear sight for the Glock pistols. The big plus of the Pachmayr rear sight is that it uses the existing front sight on the pistol, doing away with the need to purchase one. The sight is available in a target, white outline, and 3-dot configuration and adjustable for elevation and windage. The price, $67.

Aro-Tek offers several versions of its Glock sights including a "Target" rear sight without any dots and a "Two Dot" rear sight that offers six different height adjustments that permits adjustment without the use of adjustment screws or the like. Cost of either is $52.

Front sights offered by Aro-Tek include the "Aro-Glow", "Target", "Night" and "White Dot." The Aro-Glow has opening on the top and side which collect sunlight, channeling it out the back dot so the sight gives an intense glow that makes the front sight extremely easy to acquire during daylight. The colors of the insert include red, orange, yellow, and green. Cost is $25 for one color of insert or $99 for a kit with all the inserts and a tool to exchange them.

The Aro-Tek Target sight has a serrated ramp for a clear sight picture; the White Dot has a single large dot in the center of its post. Each costs $16.

One of the first manufacturers to create night sights for military, police, and civilian use was Trijicon. Not surprisingly then, Trijicon offers sights for all models of the Glock pistols with the plus of having an adjustable rear sight; cost is $175 per set. Trijicon also offers fixed sights for all Glocks; these carry a price tag of $115 per set *but* require an installation tool running another $150 making them less of a good buy.

Israeli Military Industries has developed a similar series of tritium sights for a variety of its firearms. The U. S. distributor, Hesco, Incorporated, markets these as the "Meprolight" sights and they fit the Glock pistols. Cost is $95 per set.

Aro-Tek offers tritium filled "Night Sights" with a choice of green, yellow, or orange inserts. Cost is $119 per set.

Whether night sights are used on a pistol or standard iron sights, they aren't of much use if not properly zeroed. Fortunately the sights on most Glock pistols will have been zeroed at the factory and shouldn't be adjusted unless, for some reason, they are not on the mark. In the latter situation, the sights are easily adjusted for windage and—with a bit of labor—for elevation. Before zeroing, it's wise to choose the type of ammunition that will most often be fired from the gun and zero the sights with that ammunition to avoid the changes that can occur when switching from one type of ammunition to another.

With a Glock pistol that shoots low and has non-adjustable sights, the rule is to "lower" the front sight by removing metal from its top to raise the group. If the pistol shoots high, filing the rear sight's notch and top edge will lower the group. Obviously this work needs to be done cautiously since once the metal is removed, it's really tough to put it back. It's wise to have a gunsmith handle the task, though most do-it-yourselfers can tackle the job with some success.

Guns having sights that can be adjusted for elevation make zeroing an easier task. The rule is to raise the rear sight to raise the group and lower the sight to lower the group. To help out, most adjustable sights will be marked with an "E" for elevation and an arrow showing the "UP" direction needed to raise groups.

Bullet impact can be "moved" to one side slightly by drifting the rear sight; on Glock pistols this is best done by a gunsmith since the metal insert in the rear sight easily separates from the plastic. If the gun has a replacement sight that is all metal, then drift adjustments are a possibility for do-it-yourselfers employing a drift punch or wooden peg placed against the sight and lightly tapped with a hammer.

When adjusting the windage of fixed rear sights, it should be moved opposite to the direction of the change in impact desired. If, for example, the pistol shoots to the right of the point of aim, the rear sight should be drifted to the left.

With adjustable sights, moving the sight to the left moves the point of aim to the right (shifting groups to the left); moving the rear sight to the left moves the groups to the right. Usually the sight will be marked with an "L" or "R" to show which way to turn the micrometer screw to shift the group.

Lasers

A laser produces a tight beam of coherent light that travels in a straight line; a bullet's path is a shallow arch due to gravity and air resistance. It would seem like two such different paths would never come close to matching up. In fact they do, and that makes the laser useful in locating targets. Because despite the difference between the straight line of a laser and the trajectory of a bullet, both are close enough within several hundred yards to keep them within a few inches of each other when both are properly aligned.

Modern laser sights have elevation and windage screws much like those of optical scopes; this makes zeroing them to a pistol's bore simple. The shooter employs the pistol's iron sights to aim at the target, turns on the laser, and notes where its beam strikes on the target, adjusting the laser accordingly until its beam hits at the same point as the iron sights target.

Like everything else, lasers do have some disadvantages, especially in combat since the laser can be readily seen by an opponent. And in the daylight, most lasers aren't bright enough to be seen unless used with special targets—though this may be changing as we'll see in a moment. All of this means that lasers are only practical for self defense in very limited conditions, currently either indoors or during dusk and the night.

Laser sights also aren't suited to group use by military or police squads, except when only the "leader" has a laser and uses it to direct the fire of his team. Otherwise, if each person in a squad has a laser sight, it becomes almost impossible in combat to tell which aiming point belongs to whom.

Obviously great care has to be exercised with laser sights, so they are employed in the best tactical way. But within ideal operating environments, a laser sight on a Glock pistol can be very effective and fast in bringing the firearm onto target. Too, a shooter doesn't need to bring his pistol to eye level and can fire with both eyes wide open without fear of an inaccurate shot with a laser sight. All he has to do is place the laser dot on the target, keep the firearm steady, and fire.

The silver screens of Hollywood have given laser sight users an additional plus. Because heroes in action movies often have laser sights—and almost never miss the target—the intimidation factor of a laser sight is currently great among criminals who face a laser sight.

Because of this intimidation factor, almost no one is going to stand still once a laser starts flickering at them. And this fact creates a good tactic for laser users facing combat. For years seasoned gunfighters have known that most people cower when being shot at; simply firing quickly and then taking careful aim often gives a shooter a chance to get a clear second shot at an opponent who is too busy ducking from the initial report to aim. Much the same thing happens with the laser sight; an opponent starts to duck for cover rather than returning aimed fire. The added plus is that no ammunition is wasted and the shooter is actually getting closer to his target when the laser is on since there's no recoil as when the pistol is actually fired.

A laser sight isn't going to make everyone cower in terror. And as more combatants get used to seeing these sights in action, and realize that they aren't necessarily more accurate than standard sights, especially if the shooter hasn't practiced much with them, then the intimidation factor is going to drop off. But in the meantime, it's something to keep in mind and exploit if you have a laser mounted on a defensive arm.

With the introduction of solid-state lasers over the last few years in compact disc players and other equipment, designers in the firearms industry have been able to create compact, tough sighting systems that are small enough to be practical on pistols like the Glock.

Because of the potential for eye damage, commercial laser sights are limited in power by the U. S. Government; 5 milliwatts is the federal maximum. But that's all the power needed since a 5-milliwatt laser produces a dot that can be readily seen in dim light for several hundred yards—farther than the useful range of pistols. Range isn't the only factor to consider, however. While less powerful laser sights work well, many pistol shooters have opted to use full-power 5-milliwatt laser sights because the brighter beam is more easily seen in areas bordering on daylight. The larger 5 milliwatt laser sight makes the laser sight practical in brighter environments.

Most lasers aren't readily visible in daylight, in part because of their low power but also because the red wavelength is hard to see in the sunlight. As lasers become available in other wavelengths, this may change. Several manufacturers have recently introduced a "day" laser sight that shortens the wavelength down from the standard 670 nm (nanometer) wavelength of most lasers to 635 nm. While the result of a shorter wave isn't exactly brilliant in sunlight, it is visible under conditions when the standard 670 nm lasers are invisible and when shone on a reflective surface, can be seen even in sunlight, making it possible to sight the pistol in during the day if special reflective targets are used (these targets are available from most manufacturers offering 635nm lasers).

If the trend toward shorter wavelength lasers were to continue, the limitation of these sights to very dark environments might be less of a consideration, though it's doubtful that any laser with only 5mw of power will be visible in bright sunlight at any great range.

Military and police users sometimes find infrared laser sights useful. These have the added advantage of being visible only with night vision goggles, making them invisible to most opponents while being easily visible to those with the specialized equipment. In such a situation the laser sights can be employed without detection—provided an opponent isn't also wearing night vision goggles. (For a more detailed look at laser aiming devices as well as night vision gear, see *Lasers Sights and Night Vision Devices*, available from Desert Publications.)

Battery life varies according to the power of the laser sight and size of the battery supply, but most 3 milliwatt lasers will last up to 50 hours of continuous use before they need new batteries. Full-power 5 milliwatt lasers have considerably shorter battery life.

Because a laser sight beam is readily noticeable when it's in operation, good tactics dictate only switching it on long enough to acquire the target and fire. To do this, a momentary switch is used with most laser sights with the switch mounted on the grip of the pistol.

Most laser sights have momentary switches; a few have only an on/off switch. These latter sights do away with the awkward wire connecting momentary switches to their lasers, but shooters must learn to aim their pistol straight down or into the air after firing to avoid having the beam give away their position to their target when he returns fire. (It should also be noted that laser beams are especially noticeable in smoke, fog, or rain so great care must be exercised with these sights in combat environments like these.)

The momentary switch on lasers creates a few problems when mounting the system on a pistol. If care isn't taken, the wire connecting the switch to the laser can stick out, potentially ready to be snarled in brush, or extend into the slide area of the pistol, creating the possibility of a jam at a critical moment.

Shooters sometimes opt for a standard off/on switch on the laser, even though it has the tactical disadvantages mentioned above, to get away from the wire-connected momentary switch. Others try to tape the switch to the grip of the gun, discovering the hard way that most tape oozes its adhesive over time or dissolves in cleaning solvents, creating a sticky mess on the firearm. One viable solution to the problem is to use black wire wraps (similar to those used on bread wrappers) to tie the cable to the underside of the trigger guard and then mount the momentary switch to the grip with Superglue.

More permanent laser mounts can be created with epoxy putty—at the risk of damaging the gun when the assembly has to be removed for one reason or another. A few shooters have even experimented with large black rubber "O" ring washers and rubber bands with varying results. With experimentation most shooters eventually come up with a solution, though it seems that there is no really good system of mounting the momentary switch on the pistol grip at a convenient location without having wires or fasteners protrude from the firearm.

Glock pistol shooters willing to dedicate their pistol to laser use have other options not enjoyed by owners of most pistol users. Several companies have created laser systems that are so small they can be built into a Glock, with the battery pack going into the rear space in the grip or elsewhere on the gun. These systems have the added plus of not adding much weight to the pistol and permitting use of most holsters and other accessories.

One of the first such systems was the "LAW 17" conversion marketed by SK Industries. Since then, the system has been revamped and is offered by Aro-Tek as its "LAW 2000." This system places a small battery pack and pressure switch in the rear of a Glock grip and a tiny laser diode on the front of the trigger guard. Designed by Robert Toole, the system operates at 5mw and is available in both a red "night" version as well as a 635 nm red-orange daylight version. Cost is $400 for conversion of a shooter's firearm.

Aro-Tek also offers the LAW 2200fi series of lasers. These are similar to the company's LAW 2000 system but are considerably less compact. On the plus side is the fact that the laser can be mounted on the firearm by the shooter without making modifications to the receiver of the pistol.

Another "in gun" laser sight is the LaserMax "LMS-1000" system. This 5mw laser (with infrared lasers available as an option) places the entire unit inside a replacement recoil spring guide. The laser then is projected out the front of the guide, just below the gun barrel muzzle. A tiny switch on the right side of the frame fits into the Glock's right takedown lever so the laser can be switched on or off with a flick of the finger. This kit is easily installed by the shooter and costs $495.

For those wanting an "external" laser sight, there's a variety to choose from. While these aren't as compact as the in-gun laser sights, they do have the plus of being easy to remove and generally carry a lower price tag.

Perhaps the handiest removable laser sight to date for the Glock pistols is the B-Square "Mini-Laser" which boasts a full 5 milliwatts of power in a compact size, only 1.1-inch square by a half inch, and a light weight of only a tad over 1 ounce *with* its batteries and remote switch. This laser attaches to any of the Glock pistols with a universal mount that fits around the trigger guard. The Mini-Laser is available in blued or stainless finish models with a choice of either an on/off switch that

LAW 17 laser systems mounted on each of two Glock 17 pistols. (Photo courtesy of SK Industries.)

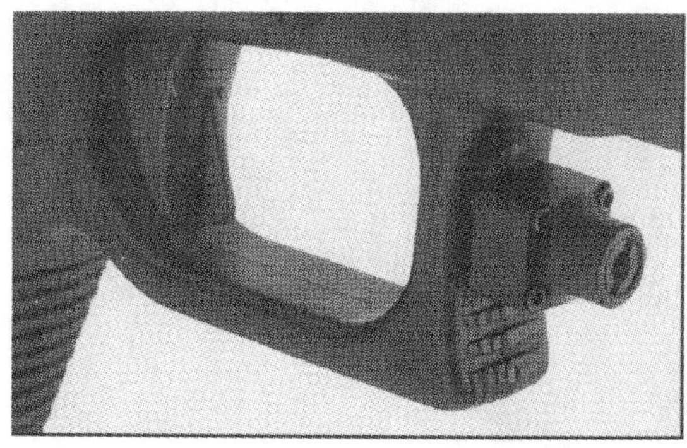

LAW 2000 MKII laser systems mounted in trigger guard of Glock 17 pistol. (Photo courtesy of Aro-Tek.)

LAW 2000 MKII laser "disconnected" from trigger guard of Glock 17 pistol. (Photo courtesy of Aro-Tek.)

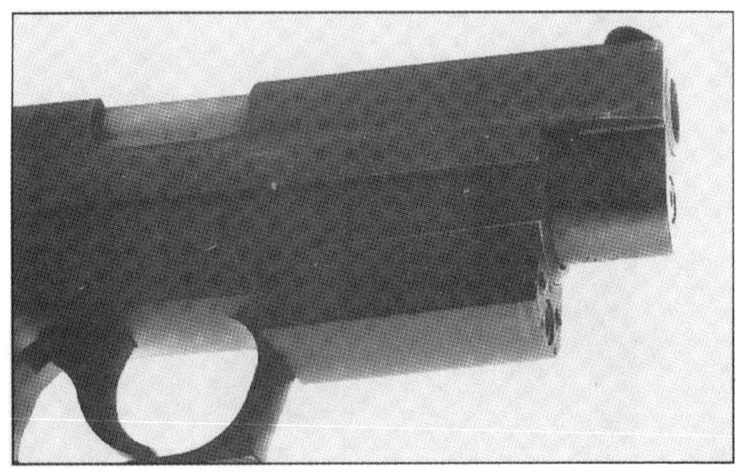

LAW 2200fi laser mounted under the frame of a Glock 17 pistol. (Photo courtesy of Aro-Tek.)

mounts on the laser just ahead of the trigger guard or a momentary switch on a cord. In addition to its compact size, the Mini-Laser has several added pluses. One is that it can be easily removed from its mount thanks to locking detentes; it's also possible to replace the batteries in the sight without removing it from the gun. These two design features make for a very flexible system that's easy to keep zeroed to the gun. Cost is $300 for a blued Mini-Laser with cord or switch and $309 for the stainless model.

TacStar Industries offers several excellent lasers including the Tac-Star "T2i" and "T1000" which are ideal for mounting

The LaserMax LMS-1000 places a laser in the spring guide of a Glock pistol. This makes for a very compact system. (Photo courtesy of LaserMax, Inc.)

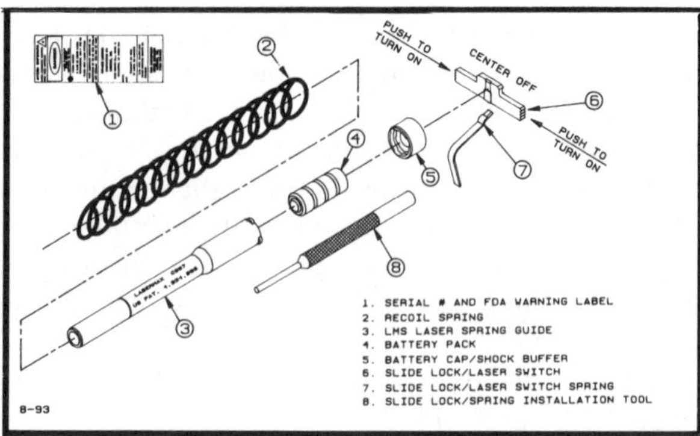

LaserMax LMS-1000 exploded diagram shows the inner workings of the laser sight as well as the slider switch that activates it. (Photo courtesy of LaserMax, Inc.)

B-Square Mini-Laser and mount on Glock 17 (Photo courtesy of B-Square Inc.)

on Glocks. These laser sights can be operated by a remote pressure switch or a rotary switch that fastens to the base of the laser for easy off/on selection with the trigger finger. The T2i is 2.43 inches long by .75 inch in diameter and weighs 1.5 ounces including its lithium battery. Its body is constructed of 6061 aluminum with a choice of black or clear (stainless) anodized finish; cost is $149.

Also available from TacStar Industries is the "Laser Pistol Mount" which can be used to fasten the T2i to Glocks as well as an adapter to mount the T2i to the mount designed for the T-1000 (below). Cost is $40 per mount.

TacStar's T-1000 is an extremely small laser sight scarcely larger than a .45 ACP cartridge, measuring 1.5 inches long and .55 inches in diameter; weight with batteries in it is only one ounce. Cost is $199.

The T1000 can be attached to a Glock with a hi-tech adhesive (which comes with the laser sight). The adhesive sets in just 60 seconds and holds up to 2,600 pounds per square inch, guaranteeing a secure attachment. However, since the mount is designed to be removed by heating it over a small flame to over 400 degrees F, this isn't the best mounting system since the heat needed to remove the base could easily damage the plastic frame of the Glock. A better solution is to use TacStar Industries' alternate mount system which clamps to the pistol, making it easy to attach/dis-attach a T-1000 to a Glock by using an "L" wrench.

ALPEC Team, Incorporated, offers the "LaserShot" and a slightly more compact "MiniShot" laser sights. Both employ a trigger guard mounting system with versions to accommodate any model of the Glock pistols. The Lasershot is 1.25 inches in diameter and 3 inches long, weighing 3.8 ounces with battery and mount; the MiniShot is 1 inch long. Both offer just under 5 millwatts of power and are available in blued or stainless finish. Cost is around $199.

ALS (Applied Laser Systems) offers the "Miniaimer" series of lasers with two wavelengths being available, one in 670nm and the other in 635nm. These laser sights are available in blued and stainless finishes with a mount that attaches to the trigger guard of a Glock pistol. Mounts cost $52 with the 670nm laser running $246 while the "day" MiniAimer (with a shorter 635nm wavelength) runs at $350.

ALS also offers a "Laser Retrofit" model designed specifically for the Glock. This laser is mounted in the forward side of the trigger guard and then uses a conventional pressure switch to turn the unit on and off. Cost is $288.

Regardless of the brand of laser mounted on a pistol, it is not a magical device that makes every bullet reach the exact spot the shooter was aiming for. To achieve accuracy with a laser sight, a shooter must practice and learn to hold his firearm steady and on target during the full pull of the trigger.

LaserShot laser sight mounted on Glock. (Photo courtesy of ALPEC Team, Inc.)

Flashlights and Flashlight Mounts

Flashlights, like laser sights, have recently "shrunk" thanks to technology. At the same time they've become brighter, with krypton or other gases making them considerably more brilliant than flashlights of decades past. As the size has decreased and the brightness increased, some shooters have discovered that placing a very compact, high-intensity light on a pistol makes sense given the fact that the majority of shootouts occur in darkened conditions.

A flashlight on a pistol helps the shooter determine who is friend or foe—something that can't easily be done with iron sights having tritium inserts or with a laser sight. Since innocent bystanders or family members can be in areas that may be invaded by a criminal, a bright flashlight cannot only identify

ALS "Laser Retrofit." (Photo courtesy of ALS.)

a target, it can be a lifesaver by giving the user quick visual confirmation of his target.

If a flashlight on a pistol is aligned with the point of aim, the flashlight can also serve as a crude aiming device, making it practical to ignore the sights when engaging a criminal at very close range. At longer ranges, the light will silhouette the iron sights, making possible targeting for very accurate shots in otherwise dark environments. Very bright flashlights even produce enough light to dazzle a criminal in the process of identifying him, giving the user a slight advantage over him.

There's a down side. A flashlight shows exactly where the shooter is and makes a dandy target. So care has to be exercised with these devices, even when they're mounted on a firearm as a sighting system. As with the laser sight, it's important to only shine a flashlight for brief periods, then move to another location quickly in the darkness. To employ such tactics, a momentary switch that can be easily activated is a must for a flashlight mounted on a Glock.

Flashlights also have a limited "range," quickly spreading out over any distance. Therefore flashlight "sights" are effective only with targets within 10 or 20 yards of the shooter with the advantage of the light quickly becoming a liability at greater ranges.

The added bulk of a flashlight on a pistol can also create problems, though the mass can also act to reduce felt recoil. And of course holster carry becomes almost impossible with some flashlight mounts (though newer, small flashlights can fit into holsters designed for laser-equipped pistols).

Currently the most ideal flashlight system for mounting on a Glock pistol is the "MicroStar T-45" flashlight offered by TacStar Industries. This bright flashlight is machined from 6061 T6 aluminum and has a black or "stainless" anodized finish and operates on three AAAA batteries which are readily available in most areas of the world. A momentary remote switch can be attached to the pistol grip for rapidly switching the light on and off; the switch can be secured anywhere on the grip with a Velcro strip supplied with the MicroStar.

It's a snap to mount the MicroStar to any of the Glock pistols because TacStar has designed the flashlight to fit its laser mounts. Cost of the MicroStar is $40 for either a black or stainless finish; the "Laser Pistol Mount" which joins the flashlight to a Glock pistol costs an additional $40 (and is also available in both stainless steel and black finish). This combination gives the buyer a very useful nighttime "tool" for his pistol for just $80.

TacStar also offers a "bargain basement" mount in the form of its "SideClip" mount that was designed specifically for the Glock pistols. This unit attaches to the trigger guard of a Glock and holds a small flashlight alongside the left side of the frame. The assembly can be quickly removed or placed on a pistol making it practical to add or delete the unit as it is needed. Cost is $20 and a mounting spacer makes it possible for the SideClip to accommodate a variety of small flashlights.

Regardless of the flashlight mount a shooter uses on his Glock, as with other systems careful practice is essential. A shooter should be able to use the light almost instinctively to illuminate his target, fire if necessary, and then avoid possible return fire by switching the light off and quickly moving to another position. Otherwise the shooter may experience a "terminal" failure of his tactics when using his Glock in a gunfight.

TacStar's"SideClip" mount, shown here with a laser sight. (Photo courtesy of TacStar Industries, Inc.)

TacStar's "SideClip" mount, shown here with a small but powerful flashlight. (Photo courtesy of TacStar Industries, Inc.)

Chapter 4

Accessories for the Glock

Many of the gadgets presently sold for pistols don't do a lot to improve the functioning of the firearm and a few lower the reliability of pistols—with disastrous results if the gun is for self-protection. Consequently the majority of shooters are better off purchasing quality ammunition and devoting their time in perfecting shooting skills rather than buying the latest gadgetry add-on for their pistol.

Among the best sources of ammunition are Olin/Winchester, Action Ammo, Federal Cartridge Company, Omark/CCI, Remington, Black Hills Ammunition, and PMC. These manufacturers offer quality ammunition that is non-corrosive (unlike some of the surplus and Eastern-European ammunition that still occasionally shows up on the marketplace). When it comes to accuracy, these companies have excellent match grade ammunition that allows a shooter to take full advantage of the precision shooting offered by these pistols. For extended practice, PMC, Winchester, and Federal all offer low-cost "generic" ammunition.

There are a few gadgets that can be worth their weight in gold to some shooters. Those engaged in shooting contests, for example, might discover that "drop-free" Glock magazines and an extended slide stop release will work wonders for their speed in reloading. And anyone who's faced an opponent in the darkness can appreciate a good set of tritium night sights or a laser sight like those covered in the previous chapter.

Regardless of the accessories a shooter elects to add to his pistol, care must be exercised because the end result may create more problems than are fixed. A laser sight, for example, may dictate a new holster to accommodate it. And that new holster might, in turn, dictate a new belt or make concealed carry impossible. The new laser might, if poorly mounted, even be in the way of the ejection port, causing what was a super-reliable pistol to become a "jammatic" when empty cartridges fail to eject properly.

One addition or change to a pistol can lead to a series of changes that can become expensive and may even lower the reliability of the firearm. This means that anyone adding accessories to a pistol or making modifications of any sort must carefully test each new configuration to make sure that nothing can go wrong at a critical moment. Failure to do such testing can spell disaster at a critical moment.

Currently there are several gunsmiths who specialize in custom work on Glock pistols. For those wanting a special modification or accessory that doesn't appear to be readily available, these are the people to check with first. Among the best are Alchemy Arms and Aerotek, though more will undoubtedly spring up as the Glocks continue to gain in popularity.

Carrying Cases

The hard plastic case that most Glocks come in is ideal for storage and even transport of the pistols. The molded box fits the gun perfectly and the hard plastic exterior gives the firearm a maximum of protection. The box can be locked and has room for the spare magazine and cleaning kit that comes with the pistol.

Some shooters will prefer another type of carrying case, perhaps because of accessories added to the Glock (like a laser sight or muzzle brake) which make it too big for its original box. In such a situation, an aftermarket carrying case may be

Top view of Glock pistol carrying case that each gun comes in.

ideal both for storing and transporting the pistol since it will protect the firearm from bumps and scratches as well as from rust and dirt. A case can also be employed for long-term storage of a firearm.

Glocks are notably rust resistant, but many accessories designed for them aren't. So it's wise to avoid using a plastic bag, vinyl pouch, or other sealed container for a storage case since these promote rust and tarnishing because air can't flow through the container. For this reason, a burlap-weave pistol "rug" is a must because it will permit moisture to escape from around the gun, heading off a lot of potential problems with rust on accessories or replacement sights.

One excellent source for such cases is Michael's of Oregon whose Uncle Mike's "Sidekick Pistol Rugs" are sold in most gun stores. The thick Cordura nylon padded foam cases have a brushed lining that won't damage the finish on a pistol. These rugs come in assorted colors including black, tan, camouflage, and forest green with the small size rug being ideal for the Glock

19 and Glock 22 and the medium size fitting most of the other models covered in this manual. Cost is $12 per rug.

Ciener .22LR Conversion Kit

Converting a centerfire pistol to shoot .22 Long Rifle ammunition has some major pluses. First off the ammunition is cheaper and second the gun can be fired in areas where full-power centerfire ammunition can't, either because of the noise generated or because of the dangers presented by lack of a proper backstop.

Johathan Arthur Ciener has developed excellent conversion units for the AR-15, Mini-14, and Colt 1911 pistol. These all work reliably and are well made.

At the time of this writing, Jonathan Arthur Ciener is slated to produce a Glock .22 adapter kit. This will consist of a replacement barrel, new recoil guide/spring assembly, and a lighter slide along with a 10-round magazine. These will all fit onto a standard Glock frame and permit it to fire .22 LR ammunition in a semiauto mode. Cost is slated to be around $190.

Compensators, Ports, and Muzzle Brakes

Compensators, ports, and muzzle brakes are most often seen on contest guns. A few are even appearing on "carry" guns these days and it seems likely that this trend will continue. Technically a compensator or gas port prevents the upward climb of the muzzle during recoil while a muzzle brake reduces felt recoil. But most of these devices actually counter both recoil and muzzle flip to varying extents. The benefits of these devices include both more comfort and quicker, accurate shooting since the sights can be brought back onto target more quickly after a shot is fired due to reduced barrel rise.

Although the Glock 17L and Glock 24C compensators don't add weight to the pistol, thanks to the cut out section on the top of the slide, aftermarket compensators generally do. And most add length as well. This latter point often dictates the purchase of new holsters to accommodate the added length and any such pistol is going to be a bit more fatiguing to carry for long periods of time.

The concept behind compensators is not all that new. John Moses Browning was using diverted gas to power his early machine gun designs in the late 1800s and the first Thompson submachine guns of the 1920s sported Cutts compensators. But the current craze for compensated pistols can be traced to the 1970s when these devices started showing up on IPSCC guns where contestants employed compensators to help bring the muzzle of their pistols back onto target in a hurry, a prime requisite for winning contests.

The first compensators to appear in the 1970s were simply longitudinal ports cut into barrels extending an inch beyond the slide of the automatic. But soon the portion of the barrel extending beyond the slide was being encased in a muzzle weight for greater recoil reduction due to the inertia of the added weight; most of these compensators were simply a cylinder-shaped weight, often with ports, wrapped around the extended barrel. More aesthetically pleasing "full-profile" compensators appeared; these followed the contours of the slide, blending with its lines.

During this same period some shooters were adding weights to the front of the frame below the slide, often with a solid block of steel being welded to the front of the frame, creating a massive assembly toward the front of the gun. Like the weight of the compensators attached to barrels, this added weight fights against the recoil of the gun.

Whether below the frame or on the barrel, as long as the added mass isn't on the slide, the "lock time" (the period of time before the barrel disengages from the slide, ejects an empty cartridge, and then re-chambers a round and locks up the action) doesn't become greater (as it would if the weight were added to the slide). This means that added weight not attached to the slide translates into a gun that can be fired more rapidly. Of course the downside to this is a much heavier gun—a pain if one has to carry the gun for long.

The latest trick gunsmiths exploit is an "expansion chamber" next to the muzzle of the barrel followed by a narrowed exit hole for the bullet. Gas becomes compressed behind the bullet and exits the compensation slots with greater pressure,

Seidler barrel compensator, mounted on Glock 17. (Photo courtesy of Aro-Tek, Inc.)

Close up of Seidler barrel compensator. (Photo courtesy of Aro-Tek, Inc.)

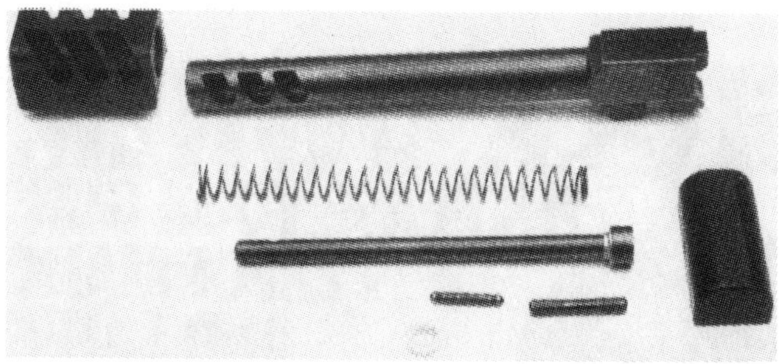

Disassembled Seidler compensator kit. (Photo courtesy of Aro-Tek, Inc.)

thereby increasing the downward deflection that operates against the muzzle rise. Gas pressure against the narrow exit hole of the compensator also reduces felt recoil in this design.

In addition to Glock's long-slide compensated models, there are three aftermarket compensation systems that are available for the Glocks. One is the Seidler Barrel-End Compensator. These units are made in Austria by inventor Herbert Seidler (of Seidler Scheiss Sport) and are imported into the U. S. by Aro-Tek.

The Seidler kits feature an extended Glock-made barrel with a Tenifer finish and which are hammer forged and use polygonal rifling just like standard Glock barrels. The big departure from the standard barrels is the addition of six ports in the top of the barrels at the muzzle end of things. These match the shroud that goes on the barrel and which is held in place with a pin.

In addition to making it possible to convert a standard Glock 17 to a compensated pistol, these kits permit shooters to just as quickly remove the system and convert their guns back to the original configuration, allowing one gun to serve both as a "carry" gun and a competition piece.

Glocks using the Seidler system do need a slight modification. Two 4mm holes are drilled in the forward end of the frame; this is performed at the Aro-Tek factory with a quick five-day turnaround. Cost of the kit and modification is $600 and the kit is available only for the Glock 17.

"Hybrid" compensator modification offered for a time by Aro-Tek. (Photo courtesy of Aro-Tek, Inc.)

Aro-Tek has also worked with the Schuemann "Hybrid Compensator" . The big plus of this system is that it doesn't add to the length of the firearm because it vents jets of gases out the top of the barrel through openings in the slide. These holes are funnel shaped for maximum "jet" action and, despite the fact that they extend well back toward the chamber of the Glock, lower muzzle velocity by only three to five percent while reducing recoil by a whopping 70 percent.

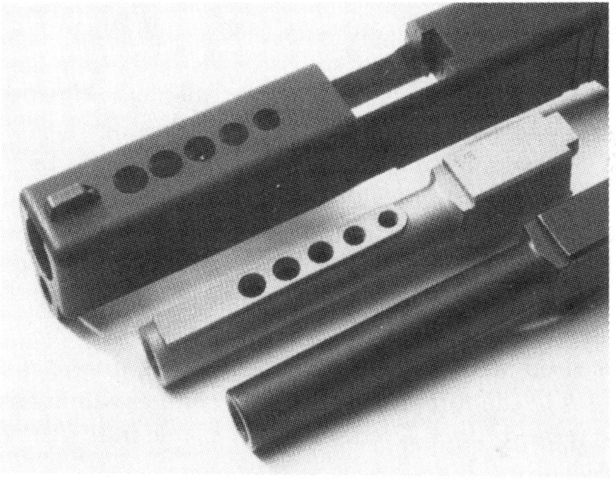

"Aro-Port" compensator currently offered by Aro-Tek uses a ported barrel (center) and slide (top). Original barrel (bottom) will still function with this system giving the buyer a "spare" for non-compensated shooting. (Photo courtesy of Aro-Tek, Inc.)

The original Hybrid Compensator used a barrel with a plate welded to its top and then machined out a section in a pistol's slide to mate with it. This worked well, but required an extensive amount of fitting and machining.

This system was abandoned by Aro-Tek in 1993 and replaced with the "Aro-Port" compensator which works in the same manner but dispenses with the mating between the barrel and a slide cutout, instead porting both the barrel and the slide. This system has the added benefit of permitting a shooter to use his original barrel with the modified slide if he decides to do some non-ported shooting (though it seems likely that few shooters would opt to go back to the original barrel given the recoil reduction of the Aro-Tek system).

The Aro-Tek compensator is available for most calibers of the Glock and black or chrome finishes are offered as options on the barrel. Cost is $300 for the modification of a shooter's gun. The system also requires that a higher rear sight be added to the firearm since the front sight is raised in the modification to the firearm's original slide.

For those wanting the "original" Schuemann Hybrid Comp barrel (and who are willing to do some machining on the Glock's slide), these barrels are still available from Brownells for $225 each with 9mm and .40 S&W barrels available in both 4- and 4.5-inch lengths.

A third variation on the compensator theme is the "Austracomp" compensator. This unit bolts onto the front of the trigger guard, extending forward over the muzzle. When a Glock is fired with the unit in place, gas is diverted out the three holes in the top and sides of the compensator. Designed for the standard Glock 17, the unit is available from Austracomp for $253.

Ear and Eye Protection

No, a shooter can't stop in the middle of a gun fight and don his ear and eye protection. But this isn't true in practice; protection will prevent hearing loss and possible eye injuries. Hearing and eye protection also helps keep flinches and other noise-inspired bad shooting habits from developing.

Ear muffs and ear plugs are readily accessible from almost any gunshop. For those who wish to shop by mail, Delta Force sells the excellent "Peltar" ear muffs which offer the highest noise reduction of most any muff.

Ear plugs must be used properly for maximum effectiveness. Most shooters don't insert expanding ear plugs deep enough into the ear canal; the secret is to roll the foam into a tight rod and then insert it far into the ear before it starts to expand.

Gross but effective "expedient ear plugs" can be created by chewing on a couple of strips of Kleenex and then stuffing the chunks of wet paper into each ear. This isn't sanitary and can cause ear infections since it gets moisture and bacteria from the mouth into the ears. But it works and is better than nothing for shooters who forget ear protectors, and discover themselves out in the field with only a Kleenex in their pocket.

Coated Polycarbonate shooting glasses are both durable and tough, capable of stopping shotgun pellets or other slow-moving projectiles. This makes them suitable for combat as well as for practice. Among the best of these are the wraparound, stylish Wiley-X from Delta Force; these are sold in clear, Hazard Orange, Neutral Slate, Blue Lunar, Silver Steel and Black Hole for $50.00 to $69.00 each. Lobos, the mirrored models are marketed as well featuring Blue, Green, Silver Chrome and Copper Mirror and sell for $39.00.

Stylish Polycarbonate glasses are also offered by companies like Jones Optical and Ame. However purchasers must always double check that the plastic used for the glasses is Polycarbonate and that it's treated to give ultraviolet protection; non-Polycarbonate glasses don't offer nearly as much eye protection.

Those on less than extravagant budgets should consider shooting glasses or safety goggles designed for protection when using power tools. These glasses can often be purchased in sporting and hardware stores for considerably less than $20—and sometimes for as little as $10. Again care must be exercised to ascertain the glasses are made of Polycarbonate and–if shooting is done outdoors–that they offer protection from ultraviolet light; otherwise the glasses may do more harm than good.

Another useful training product, "Low Lites" goggles, are like super-dark sunglasses. Shooters wearing these see things around them in daylight the way everything would appear at night or in dim light. Since most gun fights take place in poor light, police units and other groups often practice with these goggles to get the feel of tactics and equipment in darkness; such rehearsals often point out the need for different tactics and equipment and help insure success when team members operate at night. Low Lites are available from Brigade Quartermasters for $10 a pair.

Grip Panels

Grip panels on a Glock? Well, no. The molded grips of the Glock are generally seen as "Just fine, thank you," by most Glock owners. But not all.

In the past, early Glock owners improvised rubber grips by cutting lengths of bicycle inner tubes so they could be stretched over the relatively smooth grip of a Glock, giving it a better "grab" on the shooter's skin. Less effective were covers of baseball bat tape or the "bathtub" sticky cutouts that were pressed onto grips (and which one Glock owner has charitably said, "Looked like crap.") This changed somewhat with the newer Glock pistols having checkering molded into their grips — but it isn't liked by everyone either.

For those who long for the "rubberized" grips of yore but hate the improvised coverings, several companies have added rubberized sleeves that slip onto Glocks. Some shooters feel that the rubber adds a little recoil reduction and some like the added traction the rubber gives, making a hold more secure.

Each sleeve slips over the original grip of the pistol. On the downside, it adds girth to the pistol and therefore isn't ideal for those with small hands. But many shooters with larger hands love it because of its finger grooves which wrap around the front of the pistol frame, creating a very secure hold that brings the gun back on target rapidly.

Hogue offers the "Handall" soft rubber sleeve that will fit the Glock pistols. For the "chopped" versions of the Glock, Hogue also offers the "Handall, Jr." which is similar to the Handall, but scaled down for the shorter grip of these guns with only one finger swell molded into its surface. Cost of either style grip is $10.

Aro-Tek offers the "Aro-Sock" soft grip for Glocks. This is available in both a black and gray finish with both full-size and

Hogue "Handall" grip sleeve.
(Photo courtesy of Hogue Grips, Inc.)

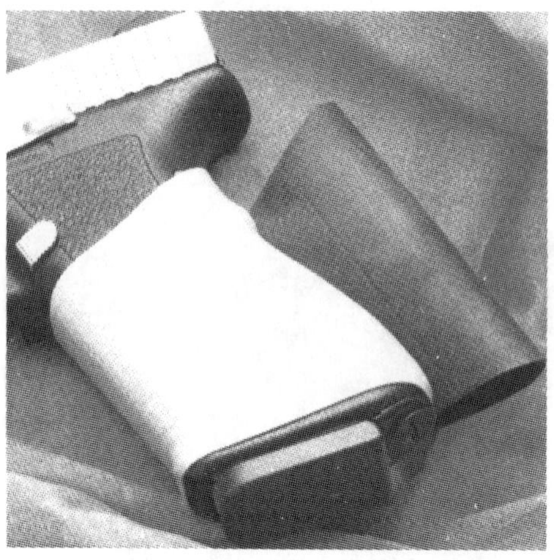

Aro-Sock grip sleeve for Glock pistols, shown here in its "silver" incarnation. (Photo courtesy of Aro-Tek, Inc.)

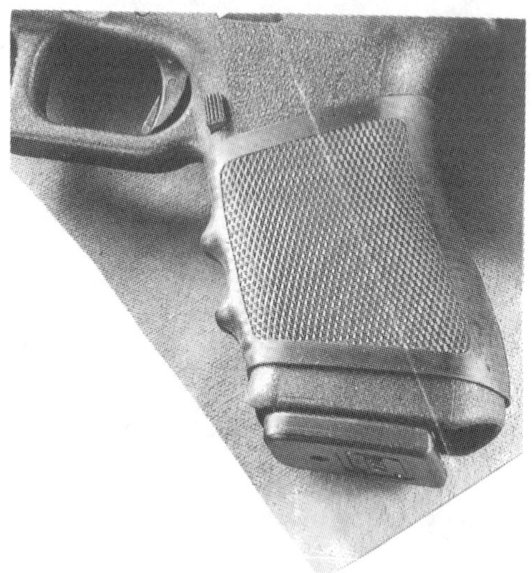

Uncle Mike's slip-on sleeve for the Glock pistols. (Photo courtesy of Michaels of Oregon, Inc.)

compact models available. The grip has a cutout in its back to accommodate the company's laser switch (though the grip works fine with non-laser-equipped Glocks). Cost is $6.

Micheal's of Oregon offers a black slip-on grip sleeve that has checkering on its side and two finger swells on its front strap. The company's full-size version of this grip (product number 59603) fits full-size Glocks while its medium size fits the compact models of the Glocks (product number 59602). Cost is $19 per sleeve.

Occasionally one also sees a "butchered-grip" Glock. These guns can vary from superbly finished to crudely ugly. The process transforms the grip angle of the Glock from its steep target style to that of the Browning High Power, SIG Sauer, Colt 1911 .45, and other older guns whose point of aim seasoned shooters may have grown accustomed to.

The alteration entails cutting a vertical slot down the hollow lower section of the grip. The two sides of the grip's backstrap are then heated and bent inward where they are joined. This decreases the angle of the grip, making the point of aim more like that of the older pistols. If care is taken, this transformation can look good; if attempted by an amateur, it is awful and there's even the potential to ruin the gun.

While the point of aim on such guns resembles that of the Browning, the feel is more "squared off" and some shooters will undoubtedly feel it's a poor substitute for either the original Glock or older style points of aim. Practicing extensively until the Glock's point of aim becomes second nature is probably a better solution than is altering one of these gun's grip.

Handi-Hider

The "Handi-Hider" from Choate Machine & Tool is a small metal bar welded to a plate with four screw holes in it. This plate can be attached to walls, under a table, or a variety of other places permitting sliding a pistol onto it, with the vinyl-coated rod slipping into the barrel. This enables a gun owner to hide a Glock pistol in a variety of out-of-sight places while still having the pistol close by, ready to be grabbed and brought into play in an instant.

Care has to be exercised to avoid hiding the gun where a child might discover it; but this system is ideal for many businessmen who want to have a gun handy in case of a hold up while not frightening gun-shy customers. And homeowners often discover that the Handi-Hider is perfect for keeping a gun close to the bed, ready to deal with a burglar. The Handi-Holder costs $7.50 with models available with 90 or 45 degree post angles and rod diameters of 9mm or .45 (which also accommodates the .40 S&W and 10mm Auto) available.

Holsters

Because the Glock pistols lack any manual safety other than that on their triggers, holsters for the Glock should be chosen with an eye toward completely surrounding the trigger and trigger guard. This will prevent any possibility of accidental discharge through a chance encounter with a branch or other obstacle that might inadvertently retract the trigger.

And of course it is essential to remember to draw a Glock from its holster with the trigger finger *outside* the trigger guard. The trigger finger goes inside the guard only when the gun is being fired.

Even more important is the cultivation of keeping the finger out of the trigger guard when re-holstering the pistol. A large percentage of all so-called accidental discharges occur with Glocks when their owners try to holster them with a finger in the trigger guard. This is especially apt to happen during moments of stress. For this reason it is essential to practice cautiously to establish the habit of keeping the finger out of the trigger guard any time the gun isn't to be fired—especially when re-holstering the Glock.

Untold pistols are carried worldwide in the so-called "Mexican Holster" (i.e., carrying a pistol inside the waistband of the shooter's pants). But just because lots of people carry guns this way doesn't mean it's ideal. This is especially so with the Glocks because of the lack of any manual safety other than that on the trigger.

Fortunately there's a wealth of holsters to choose from for the Glock. The polymer molded holsters that Glock markets

Glock's "Sport/Combat" holster makes it possible to bring the company's pistol into action very rapidly. As shown here, a skilled shooter can bring a Glock from draw to first shot in 0.4 second. (Photo courtesy of Glock, Inc.)

Glock's "Sport/Combat" holster is a carefully engineered, single molding of polymer that is both tough and inexpensive.

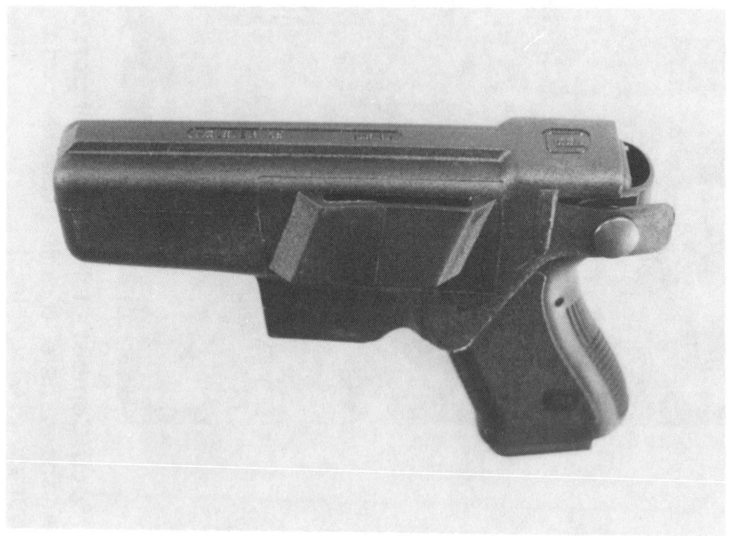

Glock "Sport/Duty" holster.

for its pistols are both inexpensive and tough. And they fit the guns perfectly. At the same time, they don't have the "traditional" look and many shooters either don't care for their look, or get tired of being ribbed by narrow-minded friends about the "Tupperware holster" they're using. That said, the Glock holsters are a bargain and should be first choice for those wise enough to adopt the best even if it is plastic. Cost is only $12 with a matching pistol magazine pouch running $7.50.

Glock's "Sport/Combat" holsters have a retention system that locks onto the trigger guard so the shooter doesn't have to fool with straps or other release systems. Shoving the pistol into the holster locks it in place and giving it a good pull releases the pistol.

The Glock "Sport/Duty" holster has a thumb break strap and is designed for a 1.75-inch belt; cost is $15.60. The "Police Holster" is actually a "Duty" holster with a plastic extension that allows the holster to hang lower on the shooter's belt. Another variation of the Duty holster is the "GI Type" which is modified to hang on a web belt with U. S.-style eyelets.

Excellent leather holsters are available for any models of Glock covered in this manual, but leather holsters are generally expensive and don't protect a firearm as well as nylon and Cordura holsters do. Consequently a shooter is well advised to first try out a holster made of these synthetic materials since they're tough and don't promote corrosion—and are inexpensive to buy. That's not to say there aren't some quality leather holsters available. DeSantis, Milt Sparks, Alessi, and Triple K all offer excellent, albeit expensive, leather rigs that are hard to beat and which are molded to fit guns exactly.

Brigade Quartermaster markets a number of nylon holsters and accessories designed for military, police, and civilian users. The company's "Quickfire" consists of a nylon holster that can be adjusted for large and small pistols thanks to a Velcro strap and an open base. The Quickfire uses a thumb break strap so a pistol carried in it is very secure; cost is $15.

Police or other shooters interested in the low-slung SAS-type holster will find Brigade Quartermasters' "Hi-Tac Assault Holster" to their liking. The flapped holster comes with all the

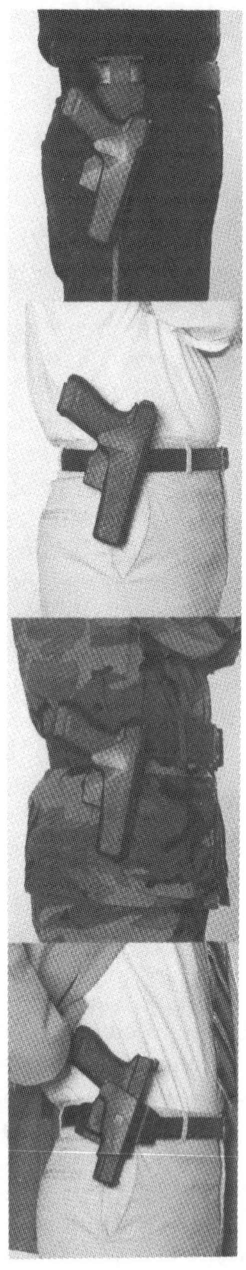

The four holster models offered by Glock include (top to bottom) the Police, the Sporty/Duty, the GI Type, and the Sport/Combat holsters. (Photos courtesy of Glock, Inc.)

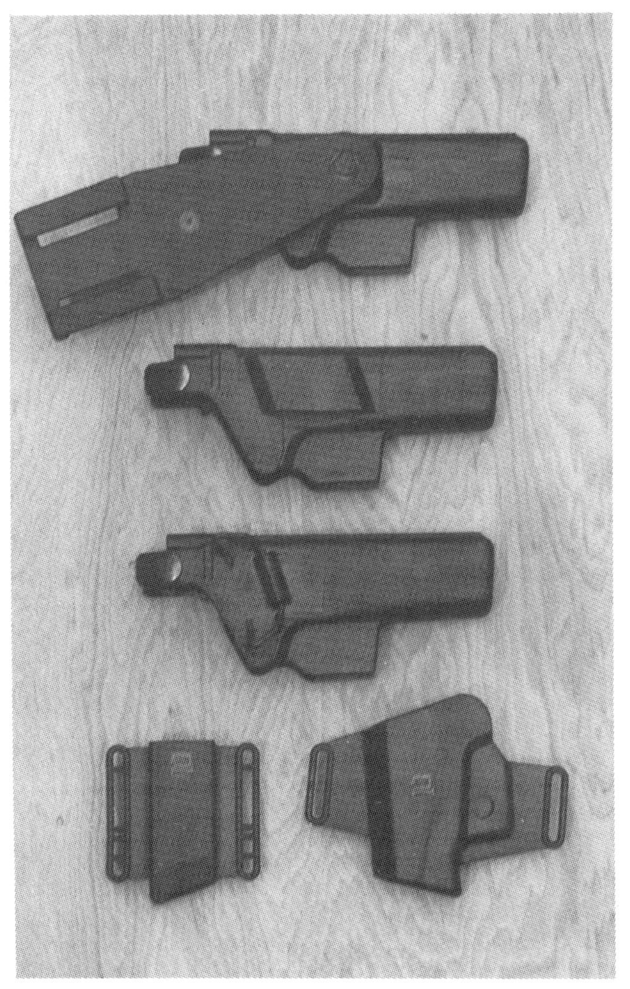

The four holster models offered by Glock include (top to bottom) the Police, the Sporty/Duty, the GI Type, and the Sport/Combat holsters (bottom, right). Also shown is Glock's excellent magazine pouch (bottom, left). (Photo courtesy of Glock, Inc.)

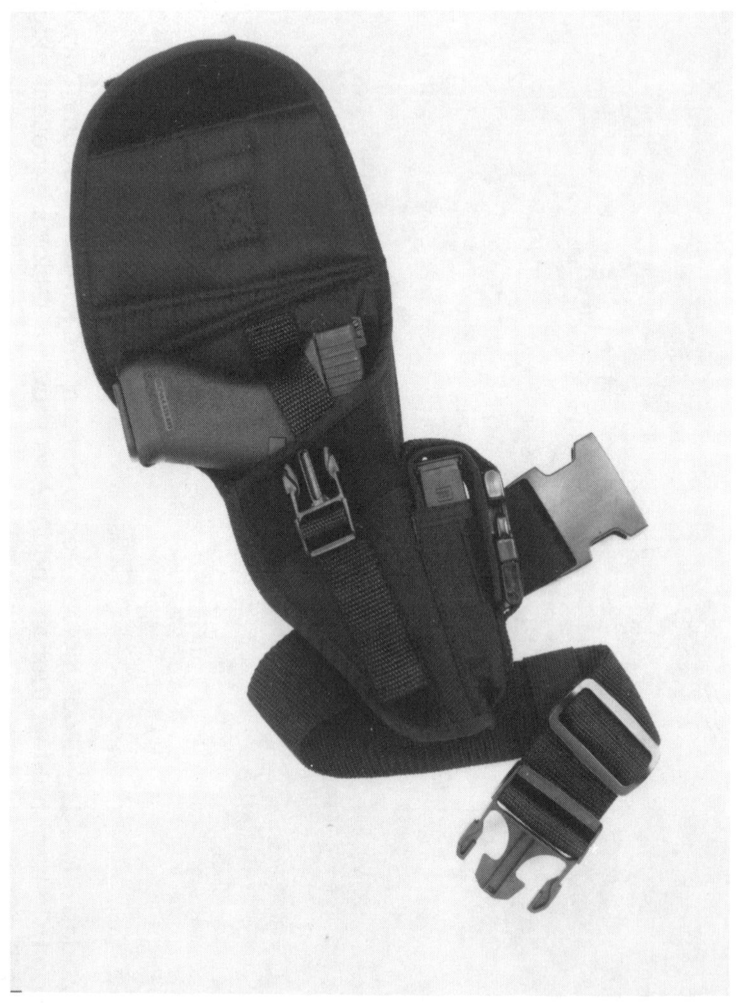

Hi-Tac Assault Holster. (Photo courtesy of Brigade Quartermasters, Inc.)

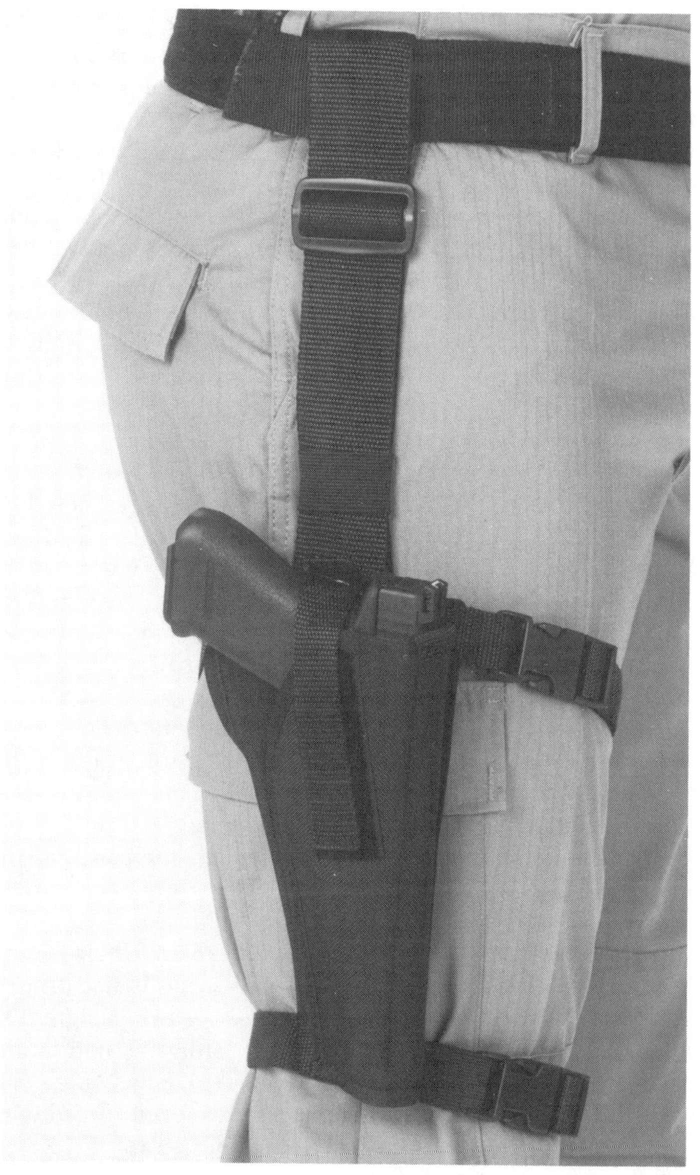

Archangel holster. (Photo courtesy of Brigade Quartermasters, Inc.)

straps needed to sling it from a belt and a secondary strap to secure it to the shooter's thigh. Fastex buckles and Velcro allow easy mounting and adjustment of the holster and a magazine pouch along its front edge makes it easy to carry spare ammunition. The black nylon pouch is padded and waterproofed; the price is $50.

Brigade Quartermasters' holster, is the "Archangel" which is similar to the Hi-Tac but lacks the front magazine pouch and flap and costs $40. For those selecting the SAS MK IV or the Hi-Tac, the company also offers the "SAS Flash-Bang Belt/Leg Pouch" which can be worn on the off-hand side, hanging from the belt and strapped to the leg to accommodate three fragmentation or smoke grenades; cost is $45.

Possibly the best bargain in the holster arena is from Michael's of Oregon in the form of their "Uncle Mike's" police and civilian holsters. Constructed of tough Cordura, these holsters are readily available at many gun stores. The Uncle Mike's belt holsters will fit onto most belts or can be worn on the company's inexpensive "Sidekick Holster Belts" designed for them. These belts have a quick release buckle making it easy to adjust and put on; they're available in brown, black, and camo. Cost is $8 apiece.

Uncle Mike's "Sidekick" holster has an adjustable snap strap to secure the gun. Sandwiched between the inner and outer skin of the holster is a thick, waterproof foam padding that makes the holster conform to the gun carried in it for a "custom fit." Available in black or camo finishes, the price for the Sidekick is $15.

For police and security guards, Uncle Mike's "Duty Holster" with thumb-break snap is ideal; cost is $30. Uncle Mike's "Duty System" series of pouches and accessories is also offered for policemen; various pouches in this series are designed to hold magazines, radios, mace, batons, flashlights, handcuffs, and keys. For the ultimate in police carry, Uncle Mike's has created the "Pro-3" line of Duty holsters; this is reinforced with plastic and has a tough thumb break retainer strap.

Uncle Mike's reversible (left or right hand) horizontal shoulder harness holster is ideal for concealed carry under a jacket.

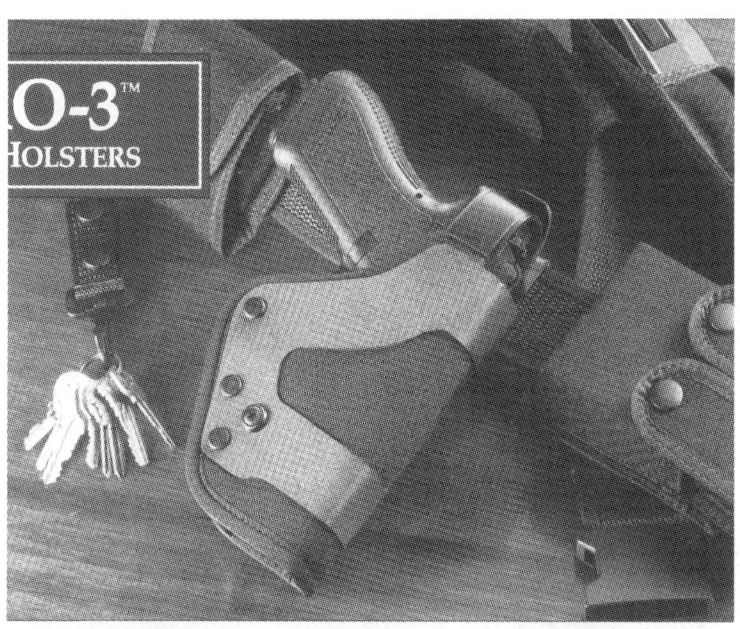

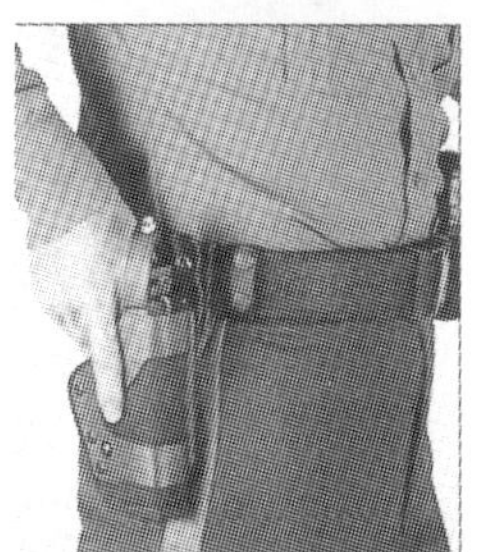

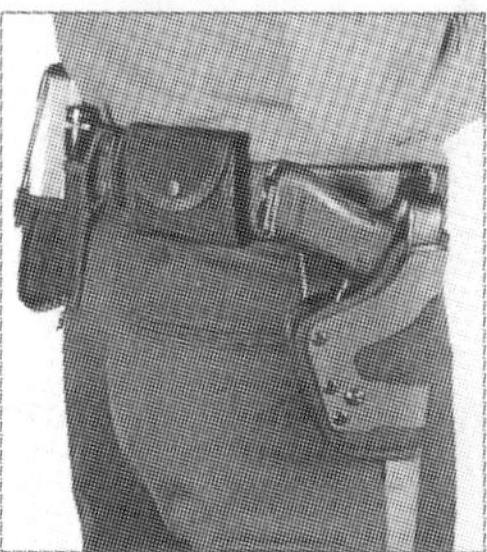

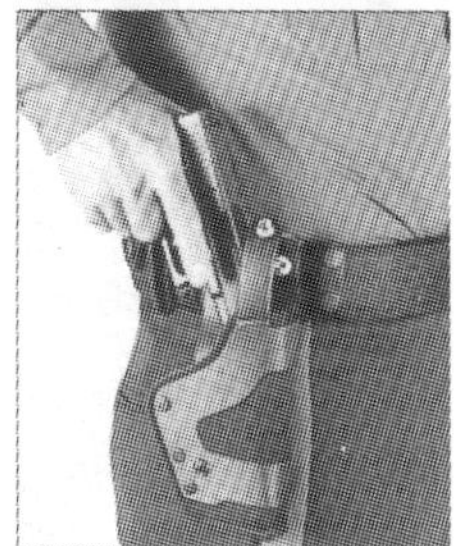

Uncle Mike's "Pro-3" holster. (Photo courtesy of Michael's of Oregon, Inc.)

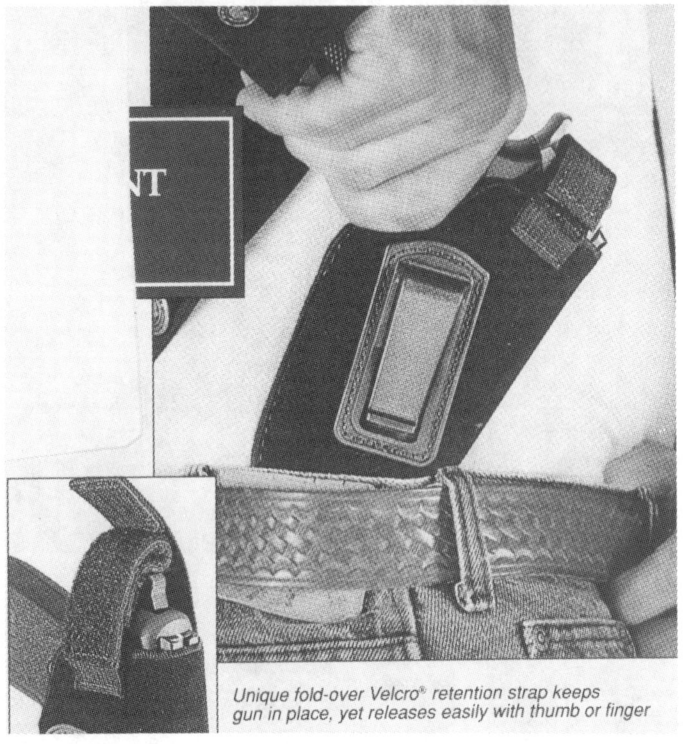

Uncle Mike's "Inside the Pants" holster. (Photo courtesy of Michael's of Oregon, Inc.)

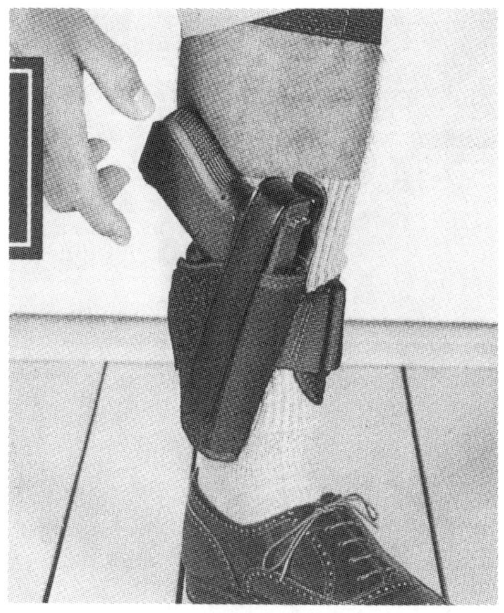

Uncle Mike's "Ankle" holster. (Photo courtesy of Michael's of Oregon, Inc.)

The "Horizontal Shoulder" with two straps crossing in the back, or the "Undercover Horizontal" using the more conventional method of looping the off-hand strap over the shoulder and back across the lower back (for superior concealment) are both ideal. Cost for the Horizontal Shoulder holster is $30 while the Undercover Horizontal retails at $25.

Concealing a pistol on a belt is considerably more comfortable than shoulder harness systems. Uncle Mike's black "Super Belt Slide" pancake holster is ideal for such carry and is offered for $18. The company also sells an ultra-thin "Inside-the-Pant" holster which clips to the belt; this holster is available in both a thumb-break and non-thumb-break style. Uncle Mike's "Ankle Holster", selling for $27, will accommodate the Glock pistols. Because of the light weight of the Glock 19 and Glock 23, they are probably more ideally suited for this type of carry than almost any other semiauto.

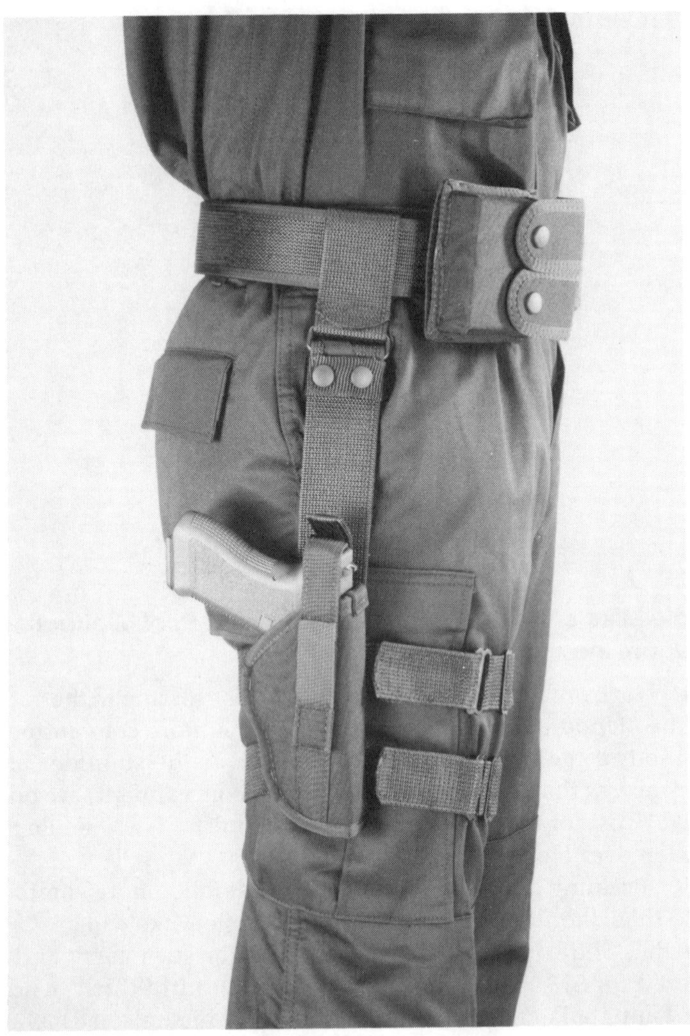

Uncle Mike's Sidekick holster with holster extension and retaining straps as well as magazine pouches and belt; all these accessories are "modular" and can be assembled to shoot the owner's needs. (Photo courtesy of Michael's of Oregon, Inc.)

In addition to holsters, Uncle Mike's single and double magazine pouches, fanny packs, and other pouches designed for hunting and outdoor use, all designed to match the finish of the company's Sidekick holsters and belts.

Shooters who add a larger laser sight or miniature flashlight under the barrel of their Glock pistol need a special holster designed to accommodate the larger bulk of the entire assembly. Fortunately two such holsters are available. TacStar Industries sells a "Universal Pistol Laser Holster" for laser-sighted Glocks. Constructed of black ballistic nylon, the "PLH-R" is the right-hand model and the "PLH-L" is the left-hand model. Both have thumb-break straps and cost $30 each.

Uncle Mike's product line includes a holster designed to accommodate an under-the-barrel laser. This holster is available in black, it has a thumb-break safety similar to that of the company's duty holster. Cost is $30.

For those needing a competition holster, things have been bleak in the past with most manufacturers aiming for majority of contestants shooting 1911-style comp guns. But this has changed with the introduction of Bianchi International's "Gilmore Speed Leader" holster which was designed by competition champ Riley Gilmore. This holster is adjustable in ten different areas, accommodating a variety of barrel lengths and styles of guns. And Milt Sparks and Alessi also fabricate comp holsters designed for contest shooting, tailoring the holster to the shooter's firearm.

Safariland has also created several "Paddle Holsters" which will accommodate scoped Glocks. These holsters are made of a laminate plastic which locks itself around the pistol. The holster itself is designed to be worn with its inner section inside the waistband, doing away with the need for a belt to hold it in place. A Belt Loop Accessory can be purchased for it for $8.50 for those wishing a more traditional carry. These Safariland holsters are available from Ed Brown Products and the cost is $47 per holster.

Several companies have come out with "butt pack" style holsters. Given the popularity of these pouches with joggers and tourists, this makes an ideal holster for those wanting to carry a pistol without alarming those around them. Care has to be exercised with these holsters, however, because pistols carried in them are considered "concealed" in many areas of the U. S. Probably the best and least expensive of these is Uncle Mike's "GunRunner Fanny Pack" style holster can conceal even a full-size Glock. The pouches even come with a badge holder for use by undercover detectives.

No matter what style of holster used, a shooter should spend a lot of time becoming familiar with it, practicing until snaps or other fasteners can be operated smoothly and the firearm presented quickly (with the finger not going into the trigger guard until the gun is on target). A shooter is also wise to always wear pistol holsters so they place the gun in the same location on the belt or under the shoulder. Switching carry positions from shoulder carry to side carry, for example, can cause a shooter to "go for his Glock" in an emergency, only to discover that it's elsewhere. Such a mistakes can be catastrophic.

Magazines

The magazine is the most significant part of a semiauto pistol in terms of reliability; damaged magazines cause most pistol malfunctions. The Glock magazine, thanks to its resilient plastic construction, is more damage resistant than most metal magazines. And the Glock magazines are very well designed and function flawlessly when properly cared for. Nevertheless the magazines can be damaged and must be properly protected. Shooters should take pains to never do anything which might scratch or alter the feed lips of a magazine, and must keep the magazine clean. A damaged magazine creates an unreliable Glock.

Because of the close tolerances between the Glock pistol and its magazines, shooters needing new magazines should first consider purchasing them directly from Glock whenever possible.

As one might expect from the "plastic gun" hysteria that accompanied the introduction of the Glock, so, too, the anti-gunners worked to limit the magazine capacity of firearms to

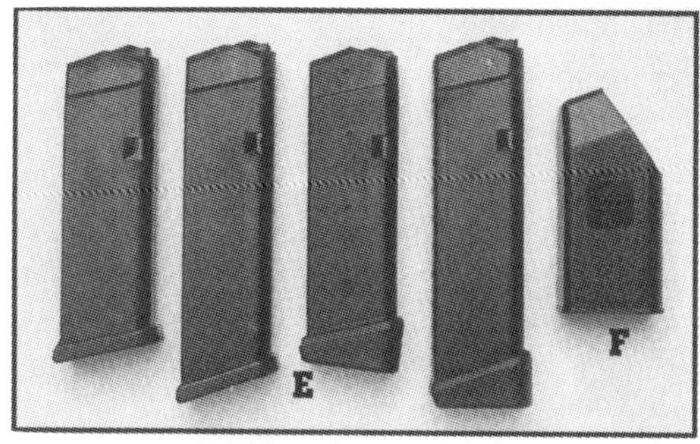

Lineup of Glock magazines (left to right (E)): Short magazine for compact pistols, standard magazine, short magazine with "+2" base, and full-size magazine with +2 base. Magazine reloading tool is shown on the right (F). (Photo courtesy of Glock, Inc.)

ten rounds; this measure became law in the U. S. with the Clinton Administration's 1994 Crime Bill. From the time the bill was finally signed into law, the manufacture of magazines with capacities over 10 rounds was made illegal, thereby assuring that only criminals would have access to new magazines after this cutoff date.

Arguably this law is a farce, given the fact that most shootings involving criminal attacks are usually over after just one or two shots (while those forced to defend themselves against a gang of criminals might need more than ten shots). But the law is the law and this one makes it harder and more expensive for honest folks to get replacement magazines for the Glock pistols, though huge numbers of them were made before the cutoff date.

There is some possible good news. At the time of this writing, it appears that the law limiting the capacity of newly made magazines may be repealed in the near future. Until the overturning of the law, however, shooters are well advised to purchase magazines as soon as they can because it is possible they may become scarce in the future.

Glock 33-round magazines shown in standard Glock 17 (left) and Glock 19 (right). Note witness holes in rear of magazine. (Photo courtesy of Glock, Inc.)

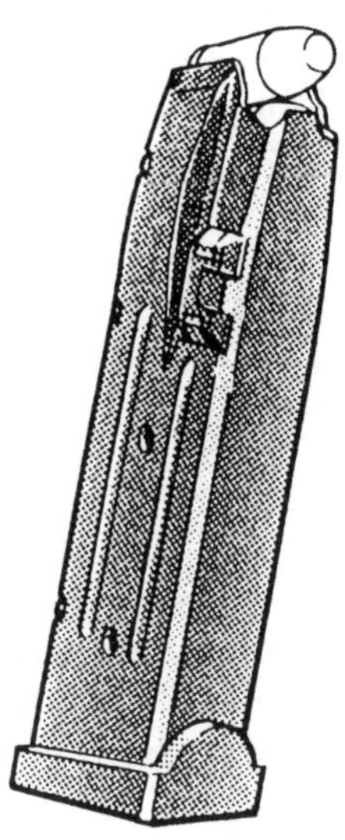

Ram-Line 17-round metal magazine. (Photo courtesy of Ram-Line, Inc.)

Glock magazines that are properly cared for last almost forever. If stored loaded for long periods of time, quality magazine springs won't get a set that keeps them from feeding ammunition reliably. Such a happenstance is rare and generally occurs only with cheap magazines or those created when a country is at war and the spring hasn't been properly heat treated. On the other hand, the polymer of the magazines does expand slightly when a magazine is loaded.

Would a Glock magazine become deformed after a long period of storage in the loaded state?

Among those familiar with the Glock, the answer is no. However many Glock owners still don't leave magazines loaded for long to be on the safe side. These people often purchase spare magazines so ammunition can be "rotated" from one magazine to another to avoid even the outside possibility of permanent magazine expansion.

Competition shooters drop magazines out of pistols to make way for rapidly inserting a full one. While this is great for speed, it can damage the magazines that are dropped. One way to protect them is to add a bumper pad to the base of the magazine. While the lightweight Glock magazines aren't too apt to be damaged when dropped, adding a weight will help insure they hit base plate first to minimize the chance of damage.

Pachmayr magazine pads are currently offered by Brownells in sets of 5 with the "MBK-59" ideal for Glock double-column magazines; cost is $15 per set of five. Contact cement is the easiest and best way to attach bumper pads to the floor plate of a magazine.

The Glock 33-round magazine is currently restricted to police and military sales. Interestingly this magazine was originally designed to hold 31 rounds and then was modified with the Plus 2 base to hold a total of 33. Since this initial design change, the magazine has always been sold in its 33-round layout.

Ram-Line offers 17-round aftermarket Glock magazines. These are made of metal and drop free of the grip when released. Great care must be exercised to use these magazines only with the company's replacement magazine release as the magazines will cut into the standard plastic release found on all Glocks. The Ram-Line magazines are available in blued and stainless finishes. Cost is $25 per blued magazine or $29 for a stainless with the magazine release costing $10. (Magazine costs are apt to go up over time due to the fact they are no longer being manufactured.)

Police and military users of the Glocks can obtain 33-round magazines directly from Glock, Inc., in the U. S.; these magazines aren't offered to civilians. However Scherer offers a variety of Glock-style magazines that have been painstakingly copied from the original Glock magazines right down to the witness marks on the back. Best of all, along with standard-sized magazines, Scherer also offers the 33-round magazine in 9mm and a similar 29-round magazine in .40 S&W. The company also sells 2-shot extension pads identical to the Glock +2 base.

Magazine Loading Tools

Contest shooters or others who regularly spend a lot of time at the range often suffer sore fingers after cramming cartridges into seemingly endless magazines. For those who need to load magazines, help has come in the form of loading tools that chuck cartridges into magazines more rapidly and effortlessly than can be done by hand.

Glock offers a handy magazine loader that comes with many of its pistols. For those who don't have one of these with their Glock when it's purchased, one can be bought from Glock, Inc., for only $2.55, making it a real bargain. Cartridges are simply

Glock loading tool positioned on magazine.

inserted into the opening at the top of the reloader which is then depressed with the free hand, pushing a cartridge downward into the magazine where it is shoved back to make room for the next round.

HKS Products, Inc., offers the "Speed Loader", a levered tool that fits onto a magazine where thumb action shoves a cartridge down into a Glock 9mm or .40 S&W magazine to allow another round to be inserted easily. The lever gives the user an added mechanical advantage and makes it possible to insert cartridges into a magazine at the rate of one per second. Cost is $10.

Ram-Line's "X-Press Loader" is a bit faster (though it takes longer to set up). This system handles Glock 9mm magazines. To use it, the shooter first places a magazine into the assembly and adjusts the bar to hold it in place. Then cartridges are dropped into the ammo hopper and a lever pulled, activating an arm that shoves the cartridge into the magazine. The X-Press Loader costs $29.97. Ram-Line also sells a "Pick Up Tube" which allows cartridges to be quickly picked up from a table top or other flat surface, aligning them so they can be dropped into an X-Press Loader; cost is $10.97.

Magazine Pouches

The magazine is critical to the proper functioning of any pistol including the Glocks; therefore it's important to carry magazines in a pouch or other container that protects them. A bump or drop on the lip of a magazine can quickly turn it into a piece of junk and some lint picked up in a pocket can cause a jam when it and a cartridge try to share space in the chamber of a barrel. The best protection for a spare magazine is to carry it in a quality magazine pouch.

Glock's magazine pouches are first choice; cost is only $7.50 per pouch making them a real steal and the pouches are tough plastic that's almost impervious to wear but which can be adopted to a variety of carrying modes.

For those wanting a more traditional magazine pouch, Uncle Mike's double magazine pouches are ideal for carrying magazines. The pouches are available in both camouflage and black and fit perfectly on the company's belts; price is $14 per pouch.

Contest shooters, especially those using Safariland paddle holsters will want to consider the Safariland "Paddle Magazine Holder" since it matches the holster and also doesn't require a belt to hold it in place, making it very quick to put on or take off. Each holder is constructed from a molded polymer that holds a magazine securely while still allowing it to be pulled from the top of the holder without unfastening any flaps, snaps, or Velcro tabs. This makes it ideal for competition, though not so suitable for self-defense purposes.

Refinishing

Refinishing a Glock is about as useful as painting a gold ring to make it last longer. Given the toughness of the frame and the Tenifer finish on the guns, most shooters are best advised to leave perfection alone.

Some shooters don't like black slides, though. For these aesthetically disadvantaged folks, help is available from

Aro-Tek will refinish Glock slides and barrels to give a variety of "two-tone" finishes on the pistols. (Photo courtesy of Aro-Tek, Inc.)

Aro-Tek. The company will refinish Glock slides and barrels in black or satin hard chrome finish. This is applied directly over the Tenifer finish and is as hard as the old finish for guaranteed wear of the pistol. Cost is $89 for refinishing the slide and $59 for refinishing the barrel.

Replacement Parts

The best source for replacement parts is Glock. Because of the close tolerances of parts and the slight variations in design that have resulted over the years, a Glock is best sent to the factory if work needs to be done on it.

Some shooters may want changes not offered by Glock, however, especially shooters engaged in contest shooting of one type or another. In such a case, having the right slide stop lever or some other doohicky might (at least in the shooter's mind) make a world of difference in how he performs during the contest. Aftermarket parts should be approached with great caution since they have the potential to make a Glock unreliable. If a shooter is depending on his gun to protect his life, then he shouldn't change its configuration. Only contest guns should be modified to any great extent and, even then, the less the better in most cases.

One part that has become popular to replace in a variety of guns including the Glock is the recoil spring guide. In theory failure of the spring guide can cause a gun to lock up. In practice this doesn't happen often and, even with torture testing of

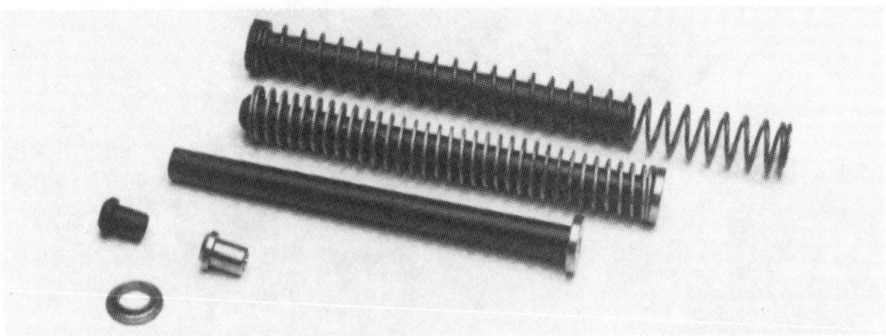

Titanium replacement recoil guide tubes offered by Aro-Tek. (Photo courtesy of Aro-Tek, Inc.)

Glocks in the 150,000 round range, this doesn't show up. All of this suggests a replacement guide is money poorly spent. That said, a guide is available for the various models of the Glock from Brownells for $37. Aro-Tek offers a lightweight titanium recoil spring guide for $32.

Owners of older Glock pistols may wish to consider buying a replacement recoil spring, guide assembly from the manufacturer. Whereas older pistols had a recoil spring that was separate from the guide, newer Glocks have a recoil spring that is captive on the guide, held in place by a washer. While this system doesn't function any better than the original, it does make it less likely that the spring will shoot out of the gun during field stripping and is therefore a useful modification. (The captive spring was first introduced on the Glock 21 and has since been used with newer versions of the other Glock pistols since 1991.)

Many shooters find the slide stop lever (sometimes called the "slide release") on the Glock too small for easy manipulation. In fact, it was designed to be impossible for a shooter to "trip" without altering his hand from the shooting position; this is an important plus since many pistols with easy-to-use slide stops have a tendency to get hung up in holsters or, worse yet, can be inadvertently pushed upward when firing the gun, locking the slide open during what was to be a string of rapid shots. So the streamlining of the slide stop on the Glocks is not without its pluses and any modification or change should be approached with a lot of thought.

Arguably the slide stop lever isn't entirely needed. When a loaded magazine is in place, simply pulling back on the slide and releasing it will permit loading a new cartridge in the barrel's chamber. Shooters accustomed to doing this could care less if the Glock's slide stop lever is as small as it is—or whether it is there or not.

But for competition shooters, things are a little different. Quickly reloading a pistol and bringing it into its ready condition dictates that the slide stop lever be easy to reach and use. And the Glock lever is just a bit too close to the frame to meet this requirement. The simplest solution for these people is to

The slide stop lever is designed to be impossible to release without altering the position of the hand from the shooting position. (Photo courtesy of Glock, Inc.)

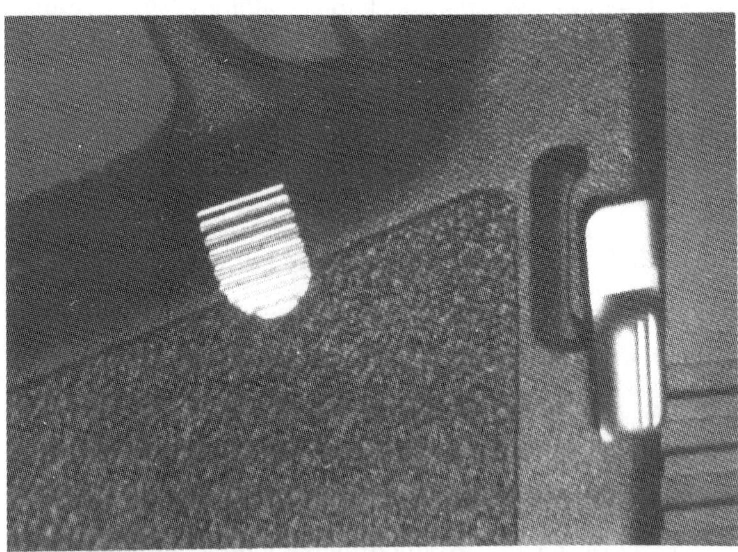

Aro-Tek "Sure Touch" slide stop lever (also shown: the company's oversize magazine release). (Photo courtesy of Aro-Tek, Inc.)

install Aro-Tek's replacement slide stop lever to the gun. Marketed as its "Sure Touch Slide Release" for $36, this stainless steel part extends out and back more than the Glock original part and makes releasing the slide a cinch. Aro-Tek also offers a matching extended magazine release, the "Sure Touch Mag-Release", for $56 including installation (and this part should be installed by Aro-Tek).

Safety

For those diehards who must have a conventional safety on a pistol, there's now a gunsmith that will do the modification. Fortunately the work isn't overly complex, thanks in part to the plastic frame of the Glocks. The work is handled by Nolan Santy at Sanco Guns. Is such a safety needed? Probably not. But there are times when such a safety might have some pluses, especially for those working close to prisoners or others who might "snatch" an officer's pistol in an attempt to employ it against its owner. In such a case an unexpected manual safety might give some precious seconds to the owner of the gun to mount a counterattack.

Underwater Firing Pin Spring Cups

This is arguably an accessory that most Glock owners will never need. Known as "underwater" or "maritime" cups, these replacement firing pin cups make it possible for water to quickly drain from the firing pin so the gun can fire and cycle properly after it has been drenched in water. Although the name of the parts suggest they enable the gun to be fired underwater, in fact this isn't too safe a practice. While the gun can be fired with FMJ ammunition at a depth of 28 inches or less without too great a chance of damaging the gun, the concussion this produces will rupture the eardrums of any shooter foolish enough to try this with his head in the water at the time of discharge. And the chance of trashing the gun is great, too. Guns aren't designed to be fired underwater and this includes the Glocks even with the so-called underwater firing pin spring cups.

Rather than an actual underwater firing device, the firing pin spring cups make it possible for amphibious troops to carry a loaded Glock and know it will function once they reach land, ideally after a judicious shaking of the pistol to get the last of the water out of its action. But pistols, including the Glocks, should never be fired underwater or with water in the bore.

That said, the author has heard stories about an elite "amphibious" military group that regularly dispatches sharks with Glocks, underwater. This may be true and might even be practical with special ammunition provided all the air had left the pistol (to prevent uneven pressure on it). But overall this would seem a very inefficient and even dangerous practice. Obviously such shooting can only be done with FMJ bullets; a hollowpoint would be expanded by the water in the bore, jamming itself in the bore. And the pressures developed by 10mm or .40 S&W would never permit such shooting which is already "iffy" at best with the 9mm.

Because of the resistance offered by water, the useful range of an underwater shot is measured by the foot. Most likely 10 or fifteen feet would be the maximum at which much damage could be done with a 9mm pistol.

The underwater firing pin spring cups are manufactured by Glock but sold only to military users, and even then a lot of paperwork has to be filled out absolving Glock of any legal liability should a shooter fire his gun underwater, damaging his weapon or himself in the process.

● ● ● ● ●

The Glock pistols are hard to improve on and, for most shooters, are perfect as they come from the box. Those intent on tinkering or needing the last increments of added capability may find that the right accessories and modifications can improve the gun for their specialized needs. But shooters must take pains to select only the accessories needed.

Accessories and modifications aren't replacements for the skill that comes with thoughtful practice. Good shooters don't get that way because of the accessories they own or the modifications they've made to their pistols; skilled shooters get that way with careful and time-consuming practice.

Chapter 5

Caring for the Glock

Glocks have demonstrated their ability time and again during military and police field tests, to cycle cartridges without problem for hours at a time. But like any other machine, Glocks will operate much better if they're given a bit of tender loving care coupled with proper maintenance. With such care, reliability problems become nonexistent and wear will be less excessive as the gun ages and the number of rounds that have gone through it climb into the tens of thousands.

Of prime consideration is proper lubrication between the various moving parts of the firearm. And not just any lubricant will do the job.

Oils designed for electrical engines or penetrating oils like WD40 are best avoided on firearms for two reasons. First these lubricants often solidify over time when exposed to the air; creating binding that causes firearm malfunctions. Second, penetrating oil is more apt than regular gun oils to deactivate the cartridge in a firearm—not too handy a happenstance whether in contest shooting or in combat.

All-purpose cleaning/lubricating solvents designed for firearms are good choices for the Glock guns. Tri-Lube, Break-Free CLP, or one of the other formulas is perfect. The shooter should oil all moving parts, taking care not to get any lubricant on cartridges or leave excessive amounts where it might run onto cartridges. With the Glock pistol no oil needs to be left on its exterior—a big plus that does a lot to keep the gun clean in dirty environments. Excessive lubricant also acts like a dust magnet, collecting grit that can become like tiny files on moving surfaces. Excessive oil can also damage holsters and stain clothing.

When lubricating any of the Glocks, special care should be taken to oil the bearing surfaces between the trigger bar and the connector. According to Glock officials, it's especially important to do this during the first few hundred rounds placed through the firearm.

How much oil does a Glock need? The Glock factory armorer's manual suggests using only three drops of oil. It tells armorers to apply the oil as follows: One drop of oil is applied to the exterior of the barrel (spread around with the finger tip); then, using the finger that applied oil to the barrel, the inside of the slide where the barrel touches has the residual oil rubbed onto it; one more drop of oil is placed on the receiver rails, again using a finger tip to spread it from one surface to the next; the third drop of oil goes to the trigger bar where it and the connector meet at the connector's angle. That's all the oil Glock recommends for lubrication of its guns.

Another option for lubricating a Glock is the new "dry lube" developed by Brownells. While the idea of a "dry" lubrication based on silicon or graphite particles is hardly new, most of these products haven't proven overly reliable on firearms, due to the temperature extremes and bizarre environments that most guns are subjected to as well as the intense heat generated by the igniting of a cartridge in a firearm.

This situation isn't true of Brownells "Action Magic II" which has been formulated with a pistol shooter in mind. After the firearm has been thoroughly cleaned, two different applications are made to its moving parts with time needed for each to dry. Once dry, the lubricants in Action Magic II actually bond with the metal of the firearm and provide lubrication without any oil that will attract dust and dirt. The chemicals

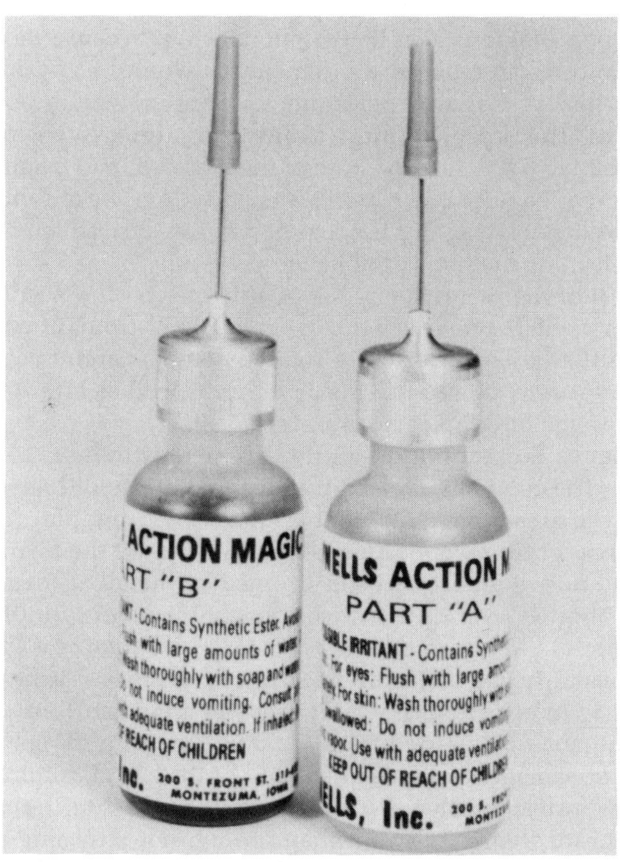

Brownells "Action Magic II" (Photo courtesy of Brownells, Inc.)

also have rust inhibitors as well as lubricants in them. All of this makes Action Magic II ideal both for very dirty environments and also does away with any potential of the lubricant to deactivate cartridges.

Action Magic II also helps with cleanup because its slick surface tends to repel dirt; often simply wiping a gun with a soft nylon brush is all the cleaning it will need, with the exception of the bore, though some shooters even place Action Magic II inside the bore of their firearm and claim that cleaning is equally quick in this area as well. (The author will confess to not trying this because of dinosaur-like adherence to bore cleaning methods established years ago.)

Cost of the two five eighths of an ounce bottles needed to apply Action Magic II to a firearm runs $16.75 from Brownells. The bottles will last for quite some time with careful use and the material is safe to use inside bores as well as on triggers, slide/frame interface, strikers, etc.

There's another important thing to note with lubricating a Glock. The company literature states that oil should never be placed in area of the slide that encloses the firing pin. Oil in this area serves no good purpose but will cause the firing pin to bind up when dirt becomes trapped by the oil or the lubricant solidifies over time (which some of the older formulas of gun oil do). *Never put oil in the area of the firing pin on a Glock.*

Cleaning a gun dictates field stripping if the job is to be done properly (more on disassembly steps in a moment). A pistol should never be cleaned from the muzzle end of things since this can damage the lands at the end of the barrel, ruining accuracy. Instead brushes and swabs should travel from the chamber toward the muzzle and then on out, not returning since that drags fouling back into the bore, defeating much of the work that's being done.

As for the cleaning kit, a visit to a gunstore will turn up a variety of cleaning kits complete with brushes sized to fit the 9mm/.357-, .40-, or .45-sized bore. Since most new Glocks come with a bore cleaner, shooters should check the pistol's case to be sure that they don't already have most of the cleaning kit already.

If time isn't a concern, the first thing to do when cleaning the bore is to send a swab or the bore brush through the barrel after soaking the instrument to the point of dripping with liberal amounts of solvent. Then the barrel should be set aside for a half hour so the solvent can really break down the dirt in the barrel.

A cleaning brush soaked in solvent is then shoved down the bore to break up the last of the fouling deposits coating the inside of the barrel. If this chore is done regularly, then buildup from metal jackets will be easily removed, saving a lot of work in the long run and also avoiding the possibility of dangerous chamber pressures produced when the bore is "contracted" in size by excessive metal buildup inside it.

Once clobbering the major grime with a wire brush, the shooter then runs cloth or paper towel swabs through the bore, again moving from the chamber to the muzzle. Some shooters prefer jags for this chore while others like the slotted cleaning tool that comes with most Glocks. Either will do the job.

Standard operating procedure entails sending a dry patch through the bore followed by a patch soaked in solvent. This alternating process continues until the patches start to come through clean. If the gun is to be stored away, the operation ends with an oil-soaked patch going though the bore. If the gun is to be loaded, a dry patch is sent through last to keep the oil from ruining the accuracy of the first shot as well as to prevent the deactivation of the cartridge by the lubricant.

Field Stripping a Glock Pistol

Field stripping is all that's needed for basic maintenance of the Glock pistol. The Glock pistols can be easily dismantled with only a push punch, but it's usually a good idea not to dismantle any firearm unless necessary for repair or parts replacement, and these guns are no exception. This is especially important to remember since there are three parts in the gun that can be reassembled incorrectly making for a potential disaster. Don't yield to the temptation to dismantle a Glock farther than is necessary to clean and care for it. And do have a

Glock-qualified armorer work on your pistol if it needs anything beyond simple maintenance work.

Field stripping is as follows:

1) The magazine should first be removed and the firearm cycled to be sure it's empty.

2) The gun is then pointed in a safe direction and the trigger pulled fully back,

3) The slide is retracted slightly (about 1/10th inch) while the slide lock levers (on either side of the frame above the trigger) are pulled down.

4) The slide is then eased forward along its tracks until it is off the frame. (If the hammer jumps forward when the slide is being pushed forward, the slide was retracted too far during the above step. Go back to step 2 and try again.)

5) The slide assembly is turned upside down and the spring guide carefully eased forward and lifted out, taking care to retain it since it's under spring pressure. The spring on early models can be removed from the spring guide; on newer guns the spring is captive and should be left on the guide.

6) The barrel can now be lifted out of the slide.

This gives the shooter access to all the parts that need to be cleaned. Further disassembly is not recommended. Reassembly is basically a reverse of this process, though the take-down levers don't need to be engaged when putting the gun back together.

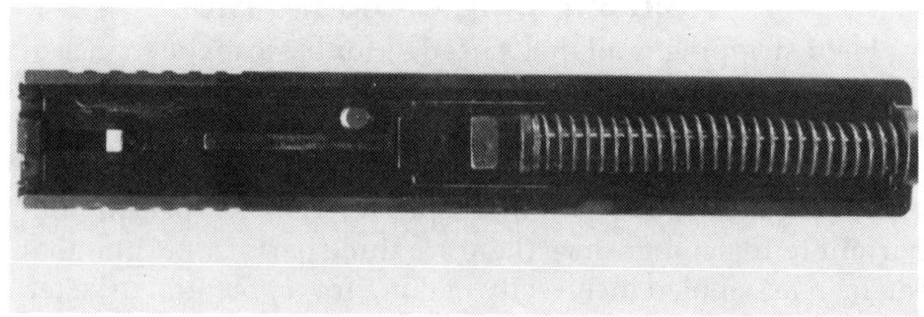

Bottom view of slide with barrel and recoil spring still in place.

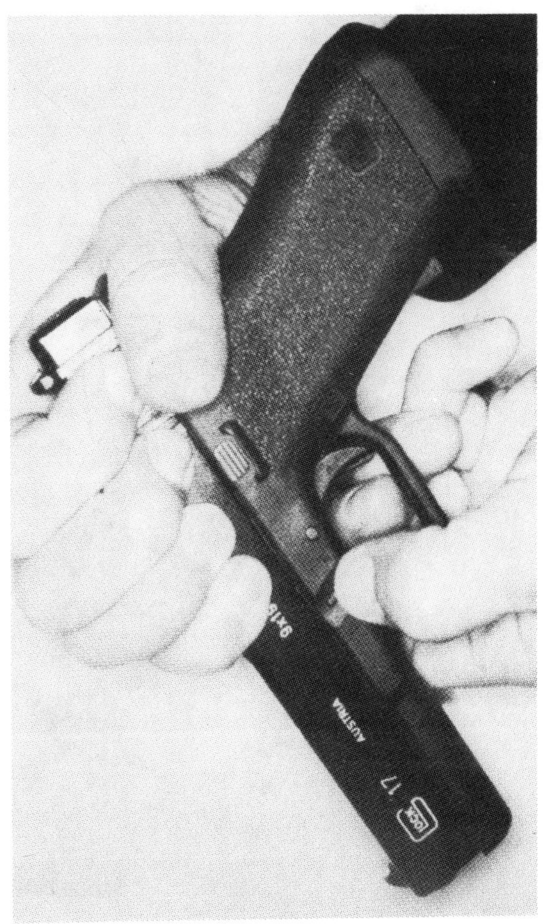

Field stripping by holding back the slide while releasing the takedown levers. (Photo courtesy of Glock, Inc.)

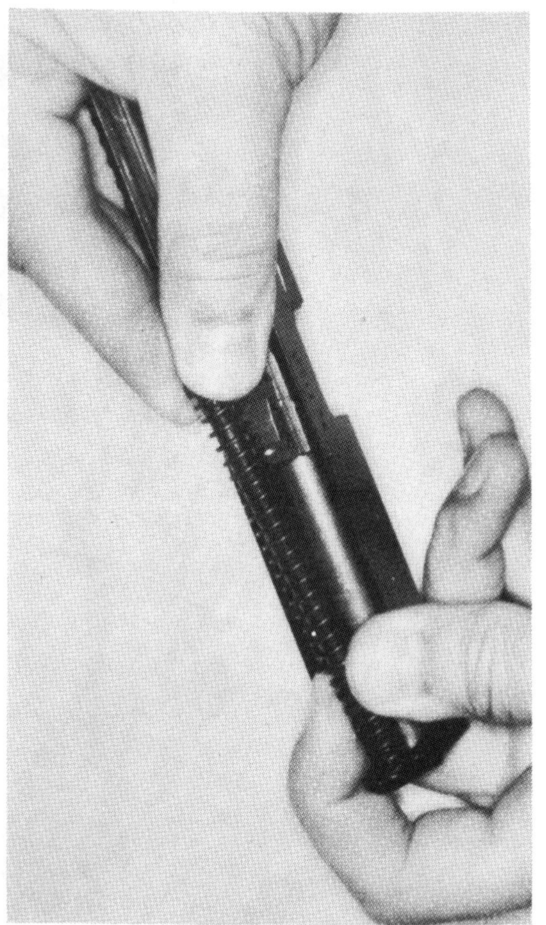

Freeing the recoil spring. (Photo courtesy of Glock, Inc.)

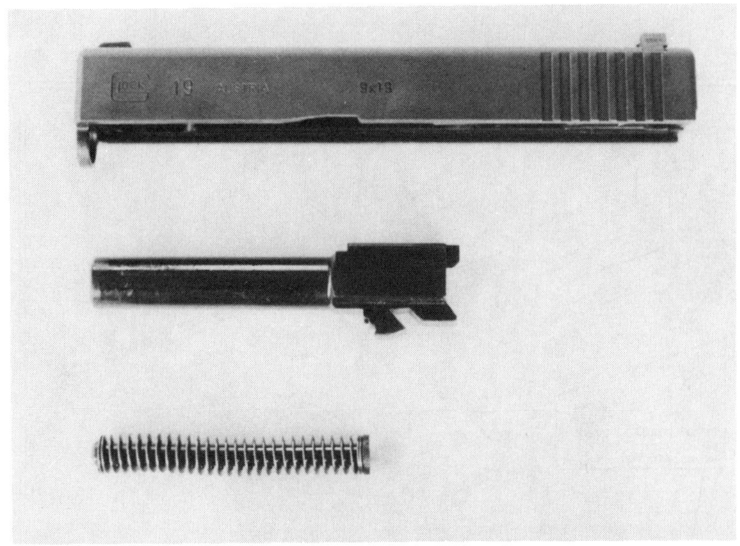

Slide, barrel, and recoil spring/guide.

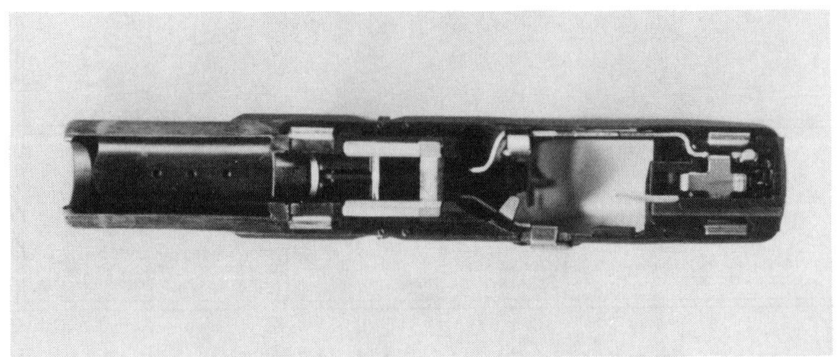

Top view of frame and internal parts.

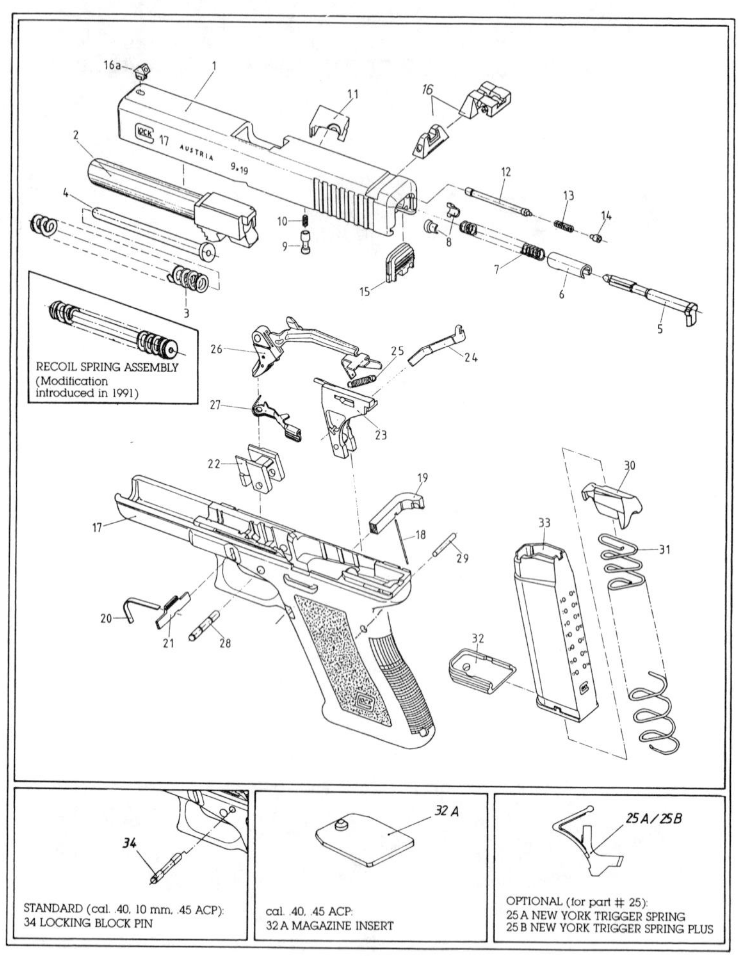

Exploded diagram of Glock pistol. (Drawing courtesy of Glock, Inc.)

Component parts for Glock pistol:

1. Slide
2. Barrel
3. Recoil spring
4. Recoil spring tube
5. Firing pin
6. Spacer sleeve
7. Firing pin spring
8. Spring cups (2 parts)
9. Firing pin safety
10. Firing pin safety spring
11.. Extractor
12. Extractor depressor plunger
13. Extractor depressor plunger spring
14. Spring-loaded bearing
15. Slide cover plate
16. Rear sight
16a. Front sight
17. Frame
18. Magazine catch spring
19. Magazine catch
20. Slide lock spring
21. Slide lock
22. Locking block
23. Trigger mechanism housing with ejector
24. Connector
25. Trigger spring
25a. New York trigger spring
25b. New York trigger spring plus
26. Trigger with trigger bar
27. Slide stop lever
28. Trigger pin
29. Trigger housing pin
30. Follower
31. Magazine spring
32. Magazine floor plate
32a. Magazine insert
33. Magazine tube
34. Locking block pin (10mm Auto, .40 S&W, and .45 ACP models only)

Disassembly of Magazines

Glock magazines as well as most aftermarket magazines can be disassembled by shoving the base plate forward and off the magazine. This frees the spring and magazine follower which must be restrained since the spring is under pressure. Great care is necessary to keep track of the follower and its spring since each part has a top, bottom, forward, and rear sides; inserting the follower or spring into the magazine incorrectly during reassembly will lead to malfunctions.

Early vintage Glock magazine bases are held in place by two tabs on either side of the magazine. By squeezing inward on either side of the base of the magazine, the base can be freed and slid forward for removal.

Since the pistol was introduced, the polymer used in making Glock magazines has been made more rigid, in part to keep the magazine from coming apart when dropped. Newer magazines have a plate that is at the bottom of the recoil spring, inside the magazine. This inner plate rests against the base of the magazine, with a small tab locking into a hole of the base. Freeing the base is accomplished by pushing inward on the tab with a punch through the hole at the center of the base of the magazine. When the tab is depressed, the base can then be slid forward and off the magazine.

With Ram-Line magazines as well as others having a "constant force" or clock-coiled spring, the removal of the base plate gives access to the inside of the magazine but doesn't free the spring or follower. With such magazines it is generally best to use some type of spray cleaner and then take care to thoroughly dry out the magazine and its spring. Pains should be exercised not to employ solvent sprays that will damage the plastic follower or sprays having water (which will promote rust). Ram-Line magazines can usually be disassembled by pushing on the locking tab on an inner place through a hole in the base plate, just as with newer Glock magazines.

Following the cleaning of the magazine, it can be reassembled without adding any lubrication to it. With metal aftermarket magazines, a very light coating of oil will aid in both the magazine's functioning as well as in rust prevention on blued steel surfaces. Excess oil must be wiped away if the magazine is to be used in the near future as lubricant can deactivate ammunition. Plastic magazines are self-lubricating and should never have oil or other lubricants placed on them, though the springs might need a light coat of oil to prevent rust in very humid parts of the world.

GLOCK®

Appendix A

Accessories Sources

AAL Optics
2316 NE 8th Rd.
Ocala, FL 34470
904-629-3211

Aimpoint, USA
580 Herndon Parkway, Suite 500
Herndon, VA 22070
703 471 6828

Aimtech Mount Systems
P.O. Box 223
Thomasville, GA 31799
912-226-4313

Alchemy Arms
501 NE 30th St.
Auburn WA, 98002.

Applied Laser Systems
2160 N. W. Vine St., Unit A
Grants Pass, OR 97526
503-474-6560

Austracomp
3947 NW 1st. Dr.
Deerfield Beach, Fl. 33441

B Square Company
Box 11281
Ft. Worth, TX 76110
800-433-2909

Bausch & Lomb/Bushnell
9200 Cody
Overland Park, KS 66214
800-423-3537

Bianchi International, Inc.
100 Calle Cortez
Temecula, CA 92590
714-676-5621

Brigade Quartermasters
8025 Cobb International Blvd.
Kennesaw, GA 30144 4349
404-428-1248

Brownells, Inc.
Rt. 2, Box 1
Montezuma, IA 50171
515-623-5401

Choate Machine & Tool
Box 218
Bald Knob, AR 72010-0218
501-724-6193

Delta Force
P.O. Box 1625
El Dorado, AR 71731-1625
800-852-4445

Ed Brown Products
Rt. 2, Box 2922
Perry, MO 63462
314-565-3261

Emerging Technologies, Inc.
P. O. Box 3548
Little Rock, AR 72203
501-375-2227

Glock, Inc.
P.O. Box 369
Smyrna, GA 30081
404-432-1202

Hesco, Inc.
2821 Greenville Rd.
LaGrange, GA 30240
404-884-7967

Hogue Grips
P.O. Box 2038
Apascadero, CA 93423
800-438-4747

Jonathan Arthur Ciener, Inc.
8700 Commerce St.
Cape Canaveral, FL 32920

Laser Devices
2 Harris Court, A4
Monterey, CA 93940
800-235-2162

LaserMax, Inc.
3495 Winton Place, Bldg. B.
Rochester, NY 14623
716-272-5420

Laser Products
18300 Mt. Baldy Circle
Fountain Valley, CA 92708-6117
714-545-9444

Michaels of Oregon Company
P. O. Box 13010
Portland, OR 97213
503-255-6890

Pachmayr
1875 S. Mountain Ave.
Monrovia, CA 91016
800-357-7771

Ram Line
10601 West 48th Ave.
Wheat Ridge, CO 80401
800-648-9624

SK Industries
1370 North Dynamics #F
Anaheim, CA 92806
714-961-1190

Sanco Guns (Nolan Santy)
River Road
Bow, NH, 03304.

Scherer
Box 250
Ewing, VA 24248
(FAX) 615-733-2073

TJ's Custom Gunworks
P.O. Box 145
Ontario, CA 91762
714-923-4422

Tasco Sports Optics
P.O. Box 520080
Miami, FL 33152-0080
305-591-3670

Trijicon, Inc.
P. O. Box 2130
Farmington Hills, MI 48018
31- 553-4960

Appendix B

Useful Information

The following books and magazines are good sources of information about current trends in the firearms industry, including those of Glock.

The 100 Greatest Combat Pistols
By Timothy J. Mullin
Paladin Press
P. O. Box 1307
Boulder, CO 80306-1307

Cartridges of the World
By Frank C. Barnes
4092 Commercial Ave.
Northbrook, IL 60062

Glock: The New Wave in Combat Handguns
By Peter Alan Kasler
Paladin Press
P. O. Box 1307
Boulder, CO 80306-1307

Handgun Stopping Power
By Evan P Marshall and Edwin J. Sanow
Paladin Press
P. O. Box 1307
Boulder, CO 80306-1307

Military Small Arms of the 20th Century (6th Edition)
Ivan V. Hogg and John Weeks
4092 Commercial Ave.
Northbrook, IL 60062

Pistols of the World
By Ian V. Hogg and John Weeks
Presidio Press
1114 Irwin St.
San Rafael, CA 9490

American Firearms Industry (Monthly magazine)
2455 E. Sunrise Blvd.
Ft. Lauderdale, FL 33304

American Rifleman (Monthly magazine)
National Rifle Association
1600 Rhode Island Ave., NW
Washington, DC 20036

Combat Handguns (Monthly magazine)
1115 Broadway
New York, NY 10010

Gun Digest (Yearly, book format)
DBI Books, Inc.
One Northfield Plaza
Northfield, IL 60093

Guns & Ammo (Monthly magazine)
P.O. Box 51214
Boulder, CO 80323-1214

SWAT (Monthly Magazine)
LFP, Inc.
9171 Wilshire Blvd., Suite 300
Beverly Hills, CA 90210

The following videos are excellent sources of information about shooting techniques which can be applied to the Glock guns:

Basic Guide to Handguns
By Jeff Cooper
Mail Order Videos
7888 Ostrow St., Suite A.
San Diego, CA 92111

IPSC Secrets
By Brian Enos and Lenny Magill
Mail Order Videos
7888 Ostrow St., Suite A.
San Diego, CA 92111

Mail Order Videos
7888 Ostrow St., Suite A.
San Diego, CA 92111

Pistol Masters
By Rob Leatham (with Brian Enos,
J. Michael Plaxco, and others)

Secrets of Gunfighting: Israeli Style
By Eugene Sockut
Paladin Press
P. O. Box 1307
Boulder, CO 80306-1307

The Glock pistols are new enough to make even the "old" models rather inexpensive to purchase. Coupled with the variety of models and growing popularity of the guns, there's an ever increasing number of people collecting these firearms. Little wonder, then, that there is now a collector's group devoted to these pistols.

Glock Collectors Association
Box 840
Park Hills, MO 63601 314-431-7878

To say that the Glock pistols are high-tech and popular would be an understatement. Glock, Inc., and Glock fans have even created a "Web Site" on the Internet. This area permits a user to download graphics of Glock pistols, see the answers to FAQs (Frequently Asked Questions), and even look through an electronic Glock manual written by John Leveron (and which had a lot of useful information that would find its way into this book).

The site also gives updates about new Glock products coming out and can even receive "E-mail" of questions from users. This is the first such operation started by a firearms company; chances are it won't be the last. The site is apparently the brainchild of Steve Tretakis, NE Regional Sales Manager, Glock Inc.; he also runs the site and often answers users questions with a personal note.

http://www.best.com/~jdnails/glock.html